TRAIN
YOUR
DOG

TRAIN
YOUR
DOG

DON HARPER

NEW
BURLINGTON
BOOKS

A QUINTET BOOK

Published by New Burlington Books
6 Blundell Street
London N7 9BH

Reprinted 1995

ISBN 1-85348-327-3

This book was designed and produced by
Quintet Publishing Limited
6 Blundell Street
London N7 9BH

Creative Director: Terry Jeavons
Designers: Terry Jeavons, Wayne Blades
Project Editors: Damian Thompson, Sally Harper
Editor: Olivia Landry
Illustrator: Rob Shone
Photographers: Norvia Behling, Kent Dannen,
Marc Henrie

Typeset in Great Britain by
Central Southern Typesetters, Eastbourne
Manufactured in Singapore by
Chroma Graphics (Overseas) Pte. Ltd.
Printed in China by
Leefung-Asco Printers Limited

CONTENTS

ONE
BEFORE GETTING A DOG

BEFORE GETTING A DOG

Owning a dog should be a great source of enjoyment, but not everyone appreciates that it is a responsibility as well. Most dogs live for about 10 years on average, and during their lives they will come into contact with possibly hundreds of people and other dogs, as well as other animals such as cats and horses. Each encounter represents a potential flashpoint unless your dog is properly trained.

Why training is necessary

Many people do get bitten, some even fatally, by dogs which have not been taught to behave properly. Children are particularly at risk, and can be scarred for life from a serious encounter. In Britain alone, it has been calculated that about 200,000 people may be bitten by dogs each year. Even more alarming is that over a

RIGHT
Always approach any stray dog with caution – it might be injured and could resent your attention. In areas where rabies occurs, there is the added risk that it could be rabid, and might inflict a deadly bite.

third of the victims are not directly touching the dog in any way at the time of the attack, according to US studies.

A second major area of concern are the dogs which stray from home, or run off when they are being exercised and cause road accidents. A detailed study revealed that in Britain approximately 1,600 accidents caused by dogs result in human injury, with about 17 people dying each year as a direct consequence of such incidents.

Most of these accidents occur in urban areas, but in the countryside untrained dogs can be equally dangerous. They may kill 10,000 domestic animals, ranging from poultry and sheep to cattle and horses, each year. Some of these dogs will be strays, abandoned by their owners because of difficulties with them in the home. Since three out of every four owners report behavioural problems with their dogs at some stage, it is clear that probably most strays are discarded for this reason, rather than because of other factors such as family break-ups or emigration.

The law in most countries places clear responsibilities on dog owners to ensure that their pets are properly trained, and not a menace to other people or animals. Civil claims for damages are not uncommon, and in the case of a serious road accident caused by a dog, the damages awarded can be very high.

It is always advisable to take out a public liability policy on your pet, as protection if you are ever involved in a dispute of this type. Specialist animal insurance companies usually offer such cover at little cost, either separately or built into a health protection policy for your pet, or it may even be incorporated into your household insurance. Ask an insurance broker for details, or look for advertisements in the canine press. You should make sure that you are adequately covered from the start, because the likelihood of a dog running away from home is probably greatest during the first few months of ownership.

Apart from the risk of causing injury, dogs also need to be trained for social purposes. No one likes streets covered in dog excrement, or being bowled over by a powerful dog pulling on its leash. Within the home environment too, training is important to prevent damage to furniture and soiling of carpets, for example.

LEFT
As well as general dog instruction, specialist courses may be available for training gundogs, such as this Weimaraner.

BELOW
Training classes are a good way to meet other dog owners in your area, and develop new friendships. All types of dogs are usually welcomed.

Starting out

Even if you have never owned a dog before, training is not difficult, and there are plenty of people to whom you can turn for advice. Dog training clubs are run in many major towns and cities, and you can enrol for a suitable course for a small fee. One of the good things about such clubs is that they offer a range of courses, so that, having mastered the basics, you can progress to a more advanced level. Ultimately you may be able to take part in national obedience competitions.

To find the address of the secretary of your nearest club, ask at your library or contact a vet, as they generally will have this information available. If you encounter a specific behavioural problem later, it may also be worth discussing this with your vet in case a medical condition could be responsible, and treatment can be provided. The distressing condition of coprophagy, when the dog consumes its excrement, is just such a case.

Canine behavioural problems are well recognized, and a specialist in this field may also be able to help you with a specific concern.

RIGHT
Training reinforces the bond between dog and owner. Here as part of an agility routine, a dog is being coaxed over an obstacle by its owner. In time, it will learn to do this by itself, without wearing a leash.

If your vet recommends contacting such a specialist, you may well be in a position to recover the cost from a pet health insurance plan, depending on the wording of the policy.

You can also turn to a professional dog trainer, who will take your dog and train it for you. Unfortunately, this is not always as successful as it might be, largely because your dog comes to relate to the trainer's commands, and so then proves more reluctant to follow your instructions. Some trainers offer residential courses, however, where you can enjoy a holiday at the same time as training your dog under expert guidance.

Breed differences

It is an undeniable fact that some breeds are easier to train than others, and this is essentially a reflection of their ancestry. Dogs have been kept for many different purposes since they were first domesticated from wolves about 12,000 years ago. Those which have a history of collaborating closely with people, such as the retrievers and other gundogs, are amongst the most responsive to training.

In contrast, hound breeds, bred to work in packs with little individual contact with their keepers under normal circumstances, present greater problems, certainly in terms of

ABOVE
Hounds which have been raised over generations to chase game by sight rather than scent can be difficult to train. This Pharaoh Hound was originally bred to pursue game, such as rabbits.

LEFT
Some dogs prove much more amenable to training than others. It can help if you have an older dog in the household, as puppies tend to follow the example of their companions.

obedience. A retriever or pointer will naturally tend to sit and stay, whereas a Beagle or Afghan Hound is bred to run, and pursue game relying on scent or sight. The culmination of its activity is at the kill, whereas a retriever needs to wait and relate closely to its owner, if it is to be successful at its task.

Other temperamental differences influence the training of dogs. Those breeds developed for guarding purposes, such as the Rottweiler, are naturally bold, and less amenable to accepting instructions from people than companion dogs such as the Tibetan Terrier which has been kept for centuries in the domestic environment.

Before you choose a breed, therefore, consider its suitability for your individual circumstances carefully. Factors such as the amount of exercise required are important, because if the dog does not receive adequate exercise it is likely to become destructive and bored around the house. As a general guide, a large dog requires more exercise than a smaller one.

It is obviously much harder to establish an indication of the eventual size and temperament of a cross-bred (mongrel) dog, compared with a pedigree (pure-bred) animal, and so you will need to try to discover the parentage of a puppy of this type. Failing all else, its feet will provide some indication of its ultimate adult size. A cross-bred puppy with large feet is likely to grow into a big dog.

Choosing a dog

Although it is always very tempting to think of taking on a dog from a rescue centre, so offering it a good home, this can prove problematic in the long term, unless you know

the dog's background. Sadly, some dogs pass through several homes in quite rapid succession, possibly because they have not been house-trained or may be highly-strung and bark continually.

If a dog has been mistreated at any stage, it can be very difficult to win back its confidence completely. What may appear to be an ordinary action, such as picking up a slipper to put it on, can trigger an unusual response from the dog if it has been hit with a shoe in a previous home. It may cringe away, or if cornered might bare its teeth unexpectedly. While adults can cope with this sort of behaviour, it is dificult for children to be so vigilant, and they will clearly be at risk with a dog of this type.

Adult dogs do take longer to settle in a new environment than puppies in any case, but you may find a dog whose history is well known. Perhaps its owner died, and there were no relatives who could care for it.

Similarly, retired racing Greyhounds are often in need of homes, and although temperamentally these dogs are normally quite sound, it can be very difficult to persuade them not to chase cats and other smaller dogs when they are out for a walk. Indeed, they may have to be muzzled as a precaution. This is not the fault of the dog as up to this point in its life it has always been encouraged to run and chase a similar 'creature' the lure at the track.

In addition dogs such as these will have previously been kennelled throughout their lives. You cannot expect them to be house-trained and, indeed, this can subsequently prove a far more arduous task than normal. The same applies to pedigree dogs which have been kept in kennels for most of their lives. They may also have missed out on the crucial period of sociability, relatively early in life, when dogs learn about their wider environment. This can create training problems later, if a dog is not used to cars, for example, as it may be reluctant to travel in this way, or is nervous of passing vehicles.

Alternatively, there are often many puppies to choose from, and these will be much easier to train than older animals, as bad habits will not yet be ingrained.

LEFT
Especially if you are not used to fitting a check chain, take care to ensure that you put it on the right way round. Otherwise you could injure your pet.

BELOW
Remember that when you remove the dog's collar, you will also be removing its identity tag. You should fit this to the collar formed by the chain.

The use of a choke chain for training purposes is not favoured by all trainers, but provided that it is fitted correctly then it should not injure the puppy, and can prove useful in ensuring that it learns to walk properly on the leash. Remove the normal collar before fitting the choke chain, so that they cannot become tangled together. The chain itself must fit properly, because otherwise it may injure the dog's throat.

Start by measuring in a rough circle around the dog's throat and up over the ears, and then add a further 5 cm (2 in) to this figure. This is the approximate length of choke chain which will be required. It is a good idea to choose a chain with broad links, as these are less likely to cause injury.

Always ensure that the choke chain is positioned correctly. Begin by removing the existing collar, and place the chain over the head in such a way that it will slacken off when the pressure on the attached leash is slackened. If you are in doubt, keeping the puppy on your left side, and facing forwards, loop one end of the chain through the other, so as to form a circle. Then place this over the dog's head before attaching the leash to the upper free ring.

So you can be certain that you have fitted the choke chain correctly tighten your grip on the leash slightly, and then relax it. This should cause the chain to tighten and slacken in turn, but if it remains tight, clearly it is the wrong way round. Under these circumstances, the chain may cause bruising, and can even result in damage to the nerves unless adjusted.

As a puppy grows, you may well find that you need to obtain a larger check chain. Here you can see that the chain is fitted correctly. If in doubt, test it as shown here.

RIGHT
The check chain fits on to an ordinary leash, by a circle as shown here. But it should slacken when the leash is held normally.

Collars and leashes

Undoubtedly the easiest way of training is to start with a puppy, at about seven or eight weeks old. At this stage it will be feeding by itself, but bear in mind that it will not have completed the necessary course of inoculations. As a result, it will not be safe to allow it out on a leash for another month. Nevertheless, during this interim period, you can begin preliminary training, and start by fitting the puppy with a suitable collar. Your local pet shop is likely to have a variety of different collars available. It is important not to confuse a collar and a 'choke chain'. Collars are made of various materials, with leather being traditionally popular for this purpose, although nylon collars are also now widely available. A choke or check chain, on the other hand, is used to train a dog to walk properly on the leash by tightening at the neck if the dog tries to pull on it.

When buying a collar, choose a fairly sturdy design, and remember that as the puppy grows, so will its neck. The collar must therefore be adjustable, because otherwise it will press on the dog's throat, and may cause difficulty in breathing. You must attach to the collar details of your name and address, with a telephone number if possible. Then if the puppy strays it will not be difficult for anyone finding it to trace you and return your pet. You

RIGHT
Leather collars and a check chain. The engraved disc here is one means of identifying your dog, and usually a legal requirement if your dog is exercised outside the boundaries of your home.

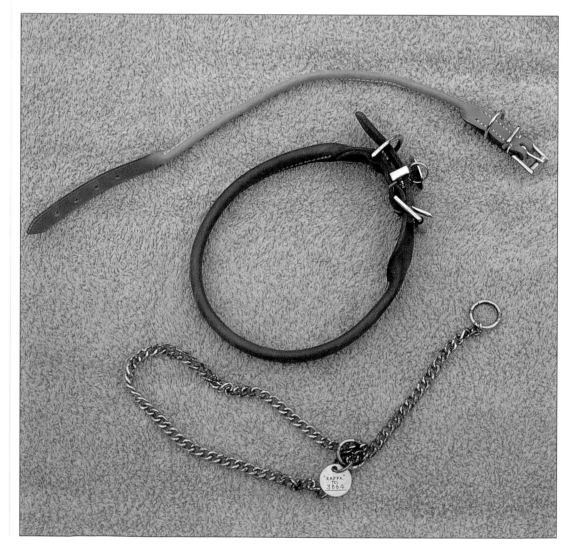

may decide to fit either a small engraved medallion or a sealed capsule, which contains these details on a piece of paper.

Another method of identification has recently become more widely accepted, in spite of the fact that it needs to be implanted surgically by a vet, although this is a relatively minor procedure. The marking device is in the form of a microchip, enclosed within a tiny container which is about the size of a rice grain. Each microchip carries a unique code, which can be read using a special scanner which is passed over the area where the chip is implanted. At present, the scanner has to be held within inches of the dog, but research work is continuing to produce an effective reading device which can be operated from a much greater distance away.

By having the individual numbers logged at a central computer, it is then possible to track down the dog's owner without difficulty. Should you acquire an adult dog from a rescue centre, it may be worth enquiring whether it is marked in this manner to ensure that the record is updated when you take possession of the dog. You will not otherwise be able to tell if the dog is marked in this fashion.

At first, the puppy is likely to resent wearing a collar, and will paw at its neck in an attempt to remove it. This phase will soon pass. When you fit the collar, you must make sure that it is not pressing tightly on the neck, as this will be uncomfortable for the dog.

A slightly different approach to prevent dogs pulling on the leash is provided by head collars, which have become widely available during recent years. These tend to be made of nylon strips with a metal loop to which the leash attaches. There is a collar component, plus a nose band which fits across the bridge of the nose.

Again, these head collars are available in various sizes, so you will need to select the most suitable size for your dog. Some are brightly coloured, and may incorporate reflective strips as well, which can be helpful if

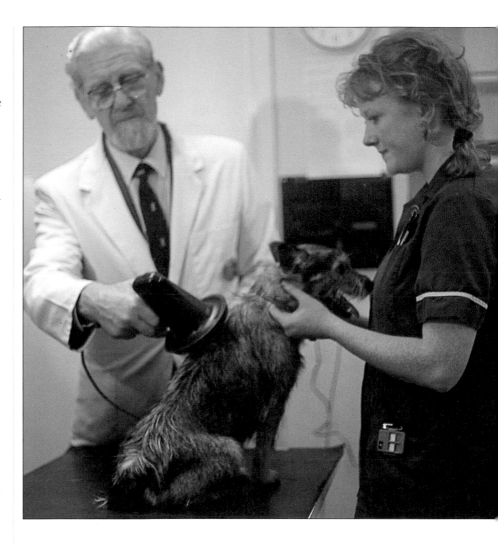

you are walking your dog after dark. They operate on a slightly different basis, controlling movement from the dog's head rather than the neck, and again, a normal collar should be removed before these are used. There is little, if any, risk of injury with a device of this type, although you will need to check that the stitching and design are suitably sturdy, as the dog may try to wrestle it off.

A wide variety of leashes are available from pet shops. Leather is perhaps most comfortable to hold for any length of time, although colourful nylon leashes have become very popular during recent years. When considering which leash to buy, check the fitting at the bottom. This must be relatively robust, yet easy to operate, since it will attach to the dog's collar.

ABOVE

Microchip implants are not a visible means of recognition. A special scanner will be required to read the information encoded on the tiny capsule under the dog's skin.

There are two basic designs, and if you are troubled by hand or wrist ailments it is probably best to opt for the sliding type of catch which can be operated by your thumb. These can be recognized by the small knob close to the base which slides the catch up and down. The other type of attachment relies upon a spring, which needs to be pressed in order to allow the loop of the collar to be secured. In either case, always check that the leash is properly attached to the collar. It is possible for the ring of the collar to become caught rather than actually restrained by the leash, which may cause discomfort.

You will also need to buy suitable heavyweight ceramic bowls to provide food and water for your dog. Stainless steel can be used, although being relatively lightweight these containers may be tipped over easily. It is important to use individual bowls which your dog relates to so that you can establish a routine at feeding time.

RIGHT
Although head collars which attach over the dog's nostrils are now widely-available in place of a neck collar and leash, they are not recommended for short-faced breeds such as the bulldog, as shown here. Aside from being difficult to fit, they may interfere with the dog's restricted breathing abilities.

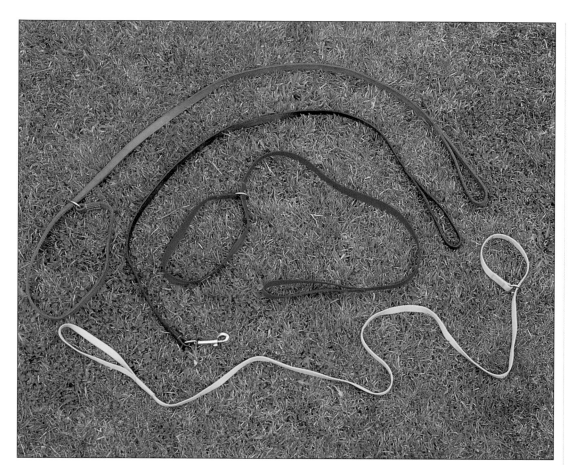

LEFT
When it comes to choosing a leash, there is a dazzling array of colours and types available. You may want to choose one with a reflective strip incorporated into the design. This will help motorists to see you if you are walking after dark.

LEFT
Young dogs in particular are messy eaters. An easy-wipe plastic mat under the food bowl is therefore a sensible precaution.

Grooming

Grooming is a vital part of dog care, and it is a good idea to train your dog to become used to this sensation from an early age. Older dogs which have not been groomed can prove very difficult in this respect.

The equipment required depends to some extent on your dog. Obviously a brush and comb are essential, and these should both be of a fairly strong, sturdy design. Nylon bristles are not to be recommended because they are likely to create static electricity in the coat and may actually damage the hair over a period of time. Metal brushes are more durable than plastic ones, while a wire brush or comb can be particularly valuable during a moulting period, removing dead hair from the coat.

ABOVE, INSET
Unless you are prepared to spend a lot of time grooming your dog, do not choose a breed such as the Afghan Hound. Short-coated dogs are obviously much easier to cater for in this respect.

RIGHT
A range of grooming equipment. Such items should always be cleaned thoroughly after use, so that parasites such as fleas or even the fungal disease ringworm cannot be transferred.

Other useful grooming tools are a hound glove, which imparts a good sheen to the coat, and a pair of scissors, necessary for trimming excess hair. Nail clippers might also be required to prevent dew-claws from becoming overgrown and curling round into the dog's flesh. These particular claws are often removed soon after birth as they serve no useful purpose. Since they are not in contact with the ground they are not worn away in the usual fashion. In certain breeds such as the Briard, they are a recognizable characteristic, however, and so need to be manicured. If dew-claws prove troublesome in other dogs, you can have them removed by your vet, although this is more of a major operation when carried out at this late stage than in early puppyhood.

Whether you intend to show your dog or not, it will need to be bathed from time to time. A towel will be required to dry off your pet, and it is a good idea to accustom a puppy to being dried in this fashion, as well as with a hair-dryer. You can obtain a range of towels which are marketed with doggy emblems.

A coat will also be essential in cold climates, especially for more delicate breeds such as Whippets and Italian Greyhounds, which have little body fat. Puppies often tend to see coats as playthings at first, and try to pull them off their backs, rolling around the ground in the process. Again, choose a fairly robust design with a neck cuff if possible. If you have a particularly sensitive dog, you can use both summer- and winter-time coats.

LEFT
Grooming is a vital part of show preparation, and dogs soon learn the routine. Here the longer hair, known as 'feathering', on this Irish Setter is being brushed to best effect.

The time needed for training

Although you will not be able to take your puppy out at once, there are many things which you can do to form a close bond between you and your new pet. But, if possible, try to involve other members of the family in the puppy's care as well, so that it integrates fully and does not develop into a 'one person' dog.

Set aside regular periods each day to spend time with your puppy, playing with it, grooming it and starting to familiarize it with

Although the first instinct is always to take the puppy to your bedroom, this is really not to be recommended. Otherwise it will be even more distressing for the dog to be ejected from your room at a later stage, when it is older. While it may be fine to have a small puppy sharing your bed, you will face a battle to remain in place if you are fighting for space with a large adult Irish Wolfhound. It is also harder to house-train a puppy under these circumstances. If the carpet in the bedroom is soiled, this will be more difficult to clear up and so the puppy is more likely to foul here again.

its collar and lead, and other equipment. Develop a strict feeding routine from the outset following the guidelines which the puppy has previously been used to before you acquired it. This will help it to settle in well.

You may have to be firm at times during these early days, especially at night. It is likely to be the first occasion that the puppy has been left on its own, away from its mother and littermates, and as a result, once you have gone to bed, it may well feel disturbed, and start to howl.

Provide a simple bed in the kitchen, such as a cardboard box with one side cut down, to give easy access, and line this with old newspaper, putting a blanket on top. Try to settle the puppy down here before going to bed. Although it may cry for a short time, it should settle down and sleep before long. Playing with a puppy for a period beforehand often helps to make it want to sleep at night.

While you may be tempted to go back to your new pet if it does cry repeatedly, try to avoid this temptation. Otherwise you are likely

ABOVE
Temperament is all-important. This elegant Borzoi is shown leaving the judging ring, calmly and with poise.

Although only pure-bred dogs can take part in breed classes at shows, there are other opportunities for cross-breds, most notably in obedience and agility competitions. In the case of breed classes, every entrant is judged not against the other dogs in that class, but rather against the prescribed 'ideal' for the breed concerned, as laid down by the governing canine authority.

Show dogs are usually amongst the best-trained of all dogs, however, irrespective of which competition they are taking part in. The dog entered regularly in breed classes will need to be thoroughly groomed beforehand, standing still while its owner prepares it for the big event. For a number of breeds, this can be very time-consuming, and calls for considerable patience on the part of both dog and owner. Then there is the travelling back and forth to shows, which can often entail a long drive.

On arrival, the dog receives last-minute grooming, before entering the ring. There will be many other strange dogs at the event, both in the ring and outside. But the show dog must ignore these, and never participate in any skirmishes with the 'opposition'. Once in front of the judge, the dog needs to display itself to best effect as it moves around the ring. It should not pause to sniff at the scents of other dogs, at the same time remaining very responsive to its owner's instructions, adjusting its stance slightly, perhaps, to show off its finer points.

Top show dogs develop a real empathy with their handlers, in the same way as horses and jockeys. But this is not enough: the judge is also likely to want to examine the dog, either on the ground or on a platform, depending on the breed and the show. Aside from running their hands

over the dog's body and legs, checking its conformation, judges may want to have a clear view of the dog's mouth, to check, for example, that the jaws are neither under or overshot, according to the breed standard. If the dog resents this, then it is unlikely to be amongst the winners.

Finally after the judging, the dog will often be returned to its bench. Each individual has its own area of staging, and obviously after a dog has done well, other owners and members of the public are likely to want to come and see the winner. Again, good temperament will be essential, as the dog is likely to be approached by a succession of strangers, in unfamiliar surroundings.

At the major shows, winners are often exposed to the glare of television lights, and expected to parade for the cameras as well, before journeying back home after a long day. This will be quite different to their usual routine, of course, when they may sleep for quite long periods.

Obedience and agility competitors face other challenges, not the least of which is performing in a strange environment. There are always distractions in and around the arena, and a steady temperament is again vital, as well as first-rate training. In order to accustom dogs for these events, there are usually classes for novices or puppies, and they provide a good basic training for bigger events. But if you are choosing a breed for show purposes, bear in mind that some breeds, for example Retrievers, are naturally more responsive than others.

RIGHT
Young dogs will readily
recognize their toys, but they
should be trained not to become
over-possessive towards them. It
is best to provide toys which can
also serve as chews when the
puppy is teething.

26

to find that your puppy will continue in this manner so as to attract your attention. If you can be firm the situation will normally resolve itself within a couple of nights or so, and the puppy will sleep peacefully.

A wide variety of toys are available to amuse your puppy. If you choose a ball,

the puppy to allow you to have the toy on occasions right from the outset so that it does not become unduly possessive in later life, as this can lead to aggressive behaviour.

One thing which will prove very disconcerting for a young puppy is to be left on its own in kennels after being in a home for

LEFT
Puppies start playing with each other even before they are weaned. When a puppy is settled in the home with you, it will soon indicate its willingness to play, even though you may not approve of the choice of toy. This situation needs to be handled with firmness yet encouragement.

however, be sure that it is large enough so that it cannot be swallowed. Retrievers are particularly keen to play with this type of toy, while all puppies like to have something to chew, especially when they are teething. Toys are beneficial in establishing the bond between you and the dog from an early stage. Encourage

just a few weeks. So avoid taking a vacation soon after you have acquired a puppy, especially if it means that you will need to place it in kennels.

If you do need to travel in an emergency, perhaps other members of the family will be able to cover for you, or failing this you may

FACING PAGE

While the big outdoors is an exciting adventure for a puppy, you will need to be certain that your back yard is properly fenced, with no gaps through which the puppy could wander further afield.

have a friend or neighbour who will be able to take the puppy into their home until you return. This will allow it to continue being part of a household, rather than being confined on its own in kennels.

Similarly, the Christmas period is usually not a good time to start with a puppy because your home is likely to be in turmoil, and you

may have visitors. You will therefore have less time to spend with the puppy during this crucial early settling-in phase.

The ideal time to start with a new dog is in the spring when the weather is likely to be improving, and with the summer months ahead, it will be a good time to start exercising and training your dog outside.

Puppies, like children, will enjoy playing out-of-doors when the weather is fine, but you should be in the vicinity to supervise the proceedings. Make sure that children always wash their hands after touching a puppy. Young dogs can be infected with *Toxocara* worms, and their eggs can be spread to people.

TWO
THE PUPPY

THE PUPPY

One of the most important points to appreciate when training a dog is that, like their ancestors, today's domestic dogs retain strong pack instincts. Consequently they look for leadership, and have a strict social order. As the trainer you must provide instructions, and the dog will accept this and adopt a subordinate role. Problems with the naturally dominant breeds, such as the Dobermann, are most likely to arise because they try to challenge your dominant position.

Dogs are very responsive animals, and the tone of the voice is one of the most powerful tools in the trainer's repertoire. An encouraging voice should always be used, except when you are displeased. Most puppies have a rather limited attention span, such is their enthusiasm for life. Training should therefore be carried out in short bursts, so as to keep the puppy interested. Choose a quiet time for training, avoiding periods when you have visitors, for example, or children are playing in the vicinity, as these will be distracting.

Some puppies tend to respond to training more quickly than others. This individual variation is quite usual, but the time taken may be a reflection on your abilities and dedication as well. It is important to adopt a consistent stance throughout. Do not encourage a young dog to jump up and greet you, for instance, and then expect it to abandon this behaviour at a later stage.

Patience is a necessary asset for successful training. Some days you will find that the dog responds well, whereas on others you may feel that you have made no progress. It is impossible to judge on the basis of a single day, however, and you should be looking for a consistent improvement over a period of time. Even so, it is important not to rush the puppy's development. Be sure to repeat the basic lessons as appropriate, so that they stick firmly in the memory.

In the case of a young puppy, one of the earliest requirements is to persuade your pet to respond to its name. The choice of name does not appear significant, although most people prefer a single word, rather than the complicated sounding names under which pedigree dogs are registered. You should repeat the puppy's name at every opportunity within its hearing, so that it becomes accustomed to the sound. This will help it to identify with you, and soon instinctively it will come to you when you call its name.

Feeding

Mealtimes provide an ideal time to use your pet's name in order to attract its attention. The puppy will be amply rewarded by responding. Although food as a reward can play a part in the training process, this should not be over-stressed. Otherwise you are likely to end up with an obese dog, and the resulting complications can lead to heart problems.

About 30 per cent of Britain's dogs are already overweight, and although it may be tempting to use chocolate drops or other treats on a regular basis in these early stages, avoid this choice. Instead, simply offer plenty of affection when your dog responds as required, and provide a healthier treat such as a small piece of carrot.

Try to feed the puppy at set times every day. As it grows older, you will probably have to reduce the frequency of feeds to one or two meals every day. These should still be kept at a regular time, because if you vary the routine too widely the dog is likely to become restless. It may then resort to thieving, or whining every time you eat, because it is disturbed with the uncertainty of its own feeding arrangements.

LEFT
Obesity is often less a reflection of overfeeding, than not allowing your dog enough exercise. Together, however, these factors can prove a lethal combination. Some breeds, like the Labrador, appear especially vulnerable to obesity.

It is often preferable to offer the necessary quantity of food as two meals, morning and evening, so the dog's stomach remains fuller over a longer period. What you must avoid, in the case of the large breeds, is offering a big meal and then taking your dog out for some strenuous exercise. This is likely to cause torsion of the stomach, which is a serious and life-threatening condition. As a result of the combination of the weight of the food in the stomach coupled with the exercise, the stomach effectively becomes twisted and dislocated. In extreme cases, this causes the dog to collapse, and although not common, rapid veterinary treatment will be required under these circumstances.

Toilet training

Feeding stimulates the intestinal tract, and it is usual for a puppy to want to defecate soon after a meal. Toilet training is one of the very earliest lessons which needs to be taught. Puppies are naturally clean by nature, so this should not prove a particularly difficult task. The basics are usually mastered within two weeks in most cases.

Young puppies do not always have full control of their sphincter muscles and so at first are not able to control the passing of urine and faeces. In any event, it is wise to place a suitable receptacle within easy reach throughout the day, and after a meal the puppy should be taken into the garden and encouraged to use an area here. Bear in mind, however, that bitch's urine in particular is quite acidic, and is likely to damage the grass of a lawn, resulting in unsightly yellow patches. Training your puppy to use a specific area of soil is therefore to be recommended from the start. Once the routine is established the dog is unlikely to vary its habits significantly as it will be attracted back to the scent.

Most owners tend to feed their puppies on the kitchen floor, placing a dirt-box nearby for use at night, or during the day in an emergency. You should encourage the puppy to go outside to relieve itself, however, whenever you are present, rather than using the dirt-box. You will need to be observant, therefore, noting when the puppy wants to relieve itself.

You can use a large plastic cat litter tray as a dirt-box. Fill this with a small amount of cat litter, having lined it first with newspaper. This will make it easier to clean once it is soiled. You will need to remove and discard the detachable lid, which is a feature of many cat litter trays, since this will just get in the way, and means that accidents are more likely to happen. As an additional precaution, you should stand the tray on newspaper.

Several manufacturers now market products which are claimed to attract dogs for toilet purposes. You can add one of these to the litter in the first instance, as it may encourage your puppy to relieve itself here.

Although it may not appear especially hygienic to keep the litter tray in the kitchen, this is probably the best place because the floor surface here tends to be impermeable. If a disaster occurs it will be easy to disinfect the area thoroughly. This is especially important in a home with young children.

BELOW
Puppies will often relieve themselves more readily on an area of short grass, rather than bare concrete. In order to prevent damage to a lawn, they can be trained to use a flower-bed.

LEFT
There will be occasions when the puppy is more interested in playing than relieving itself. Your presence may help to concentrate its mind, however, and you can establish a routine whereby it can run around and play for a few minutes after it has performed as desired.

Many puppies are infected at birth with the roundworm *Toxocara canis*, and so must be wormed frequently on a vet's advice for the first six months of life, and regularly thereafter. The eggs of these parasites are voided in the faeces, and the resulting larvae do represent a slight risk to human health, because they may cause the disease known as toxocariasis. The eggs can be swallowed by children who are apt to put dirty fingers into their mouths; the larvae may then migrate from the gut around the body. If they form a cyst in the eye, blindness is likely to result.

By thoroughly cleaning the soiled area you will prevent human infection, simply because the eggs are not immediately infective when they are passed from the dog's body in its faeces. They will take approximately a week to reach this stage, so that while any traces remaining in a carpet could give rise to problems, a solid floor can be easily disinfected to kill them before this stage is reached. The eggs can remain viable for a considerable period of time, however, and so you should

dispose of faecal matter carefully to prevent any risk of infection in the garden if you have a young family.

The threat posed by toxocariasis, or *visceral larval migrans*, as it is also known, is relatively slight with about 10 cases a year being recorded in England and Wales, as an example. Nevertheless, it is a serious condition if the eye is affected, and sensible precautionary measures should be taken. Children must be supervised at all times when in contact with puppies, and then taught to wash their hands afterwards as a matter of course.

When you first introduce the litter tray, place the puppy here if you suspect that it is likely to use it. If you have a conservatory area behind your kitchen, this may be an even better location for the tray, since here it will be close to an outer door. The aim is, of course, to persuade the puppy to ask to go outside into the garden when it wants to urinate or defecate.

After a meal, when you take the puppy outside, try the scenting preparation again, although its possible effects are likely to be diluted by rain. Point to the spot, and this should serve to encourage the puppy to sniff in this region. Although at first it may prove excitable and run off around the garden, the puppy should soon return to you. Such excitement alone may cause it to urinate here.

You can offer encouragement, using a phrase which the young dog will come to identify with in time, such as 'clean dog'. Give plenty of praise and encouragement once it has performed as you want before calling the youngster by its name to follow you back indoors. This is useful practise to prepare for the time when you allow the dog off the leash for the first time, and call it back to you.

If the puppy has done nothing after five or 10 minutes, follow the same routine, but once you are inside remain more watchful. A number of factors, such as noise, rain and even washing flapping on a clothes-line, may disturb a young puppy in such surroundings. Once it is back within the confines of home, however, it may immediately decide to go to the toilet. There is really little point in scolding the puppy at this stage, especially if it has not been used to the big outdoors before.

Once your dog has relieved itself, clean up the area thoroughly using a dog scoop. Several disposable types are available from pet shops, and are essential for dog owners where it is compulsory to clean up after their pets if they are walking in a public area. Although the area can then be cleaned, the puppy is likely to be attracted back to the site again unless you can remove the underlying odour. Dogs have very sensitive noses, and they rely heavily on scent markings in their lives.

While disinfecting the soiled area is obviously to be recommended, you need to be careful in your choice of disinfectant. This is because some disinfectants serve to reinforce rather than overcome such scents which are not discernible by our noses. Pine-scented products may do this and so are best avoided for this reason. Vinegar can be used to remove the scent, and again, products are available from pet shops which fulfil a similar function, in contrast to those which attract the dog.

LEFT
After relieving itself, a puppy may start scratching and digging the ground. This behaviour should not be encouraged, because it can cause damage to the lawn or plants. You will also need to wipe your pet's feet with a towel to remove mud before you allow it back in the home.

On average, young puppies may relieve themselves about six times a day. Under no circumstances, however, particularly when you are feeding a dried diet, should you withhold water for any period of time in order to reduce urinary output. This can have devastating consequences, and may cause long-term damage to the urinary tract. Urine production naturally declines while the puppy is asleep, so that once it has been put outside at night, then the young dog should be able to last quite comfortably through to the morning. Take it out into the garden again then, without delay.

Puppies are unable to relate to an event which occurred in the past, so if you find that a place has been soiled overnight there is little point in scolding the puppy accordingly. Nor should you rub the dog's nose in it. This is merely unpleasant, and serves no useful purpose. After all, dogs actually sniff regularly where others have soiled, around lamp posts for example, so this is certainly no deterrent.

Although the basics of toilet training can be mastered rapidly, it will take two or three months before a puppy is regularly asking to go outside of its own accord. Occasional

breakdowns in the training may not be
uncommon at this stage, and you should make
sure that the litter tray is available overnight or
if you have to leave the puppy for a short time
during the day.

Do not be too quick to blame the puppy if
it makes a mess when you are indoors. By this
stage, you yourself may be becoming less
observant and more complacent, and so
overlook your puppy's demand to be let out!

When persistent problems do occur there
may be an underlying medical reason. Actual
punishment should only be used as a last
resort; a sharp tap with a cardboard strip is
quite sufficient. Training based on
encouragement and praise is likely to prove far
more effective in the longer term.

If you are at all concerned about your
puppy's lack of progress during house-training,
then consult your vet. A weak sphincter muscle
or a congenital deformation in the urinary
system may be the underlying cause, or it could
be a digestive upset causing diarrhoea. You
should always seek veterinary advice without
delay in this case because the condition of a
young puppy can deteriorate very rapidly if it
becomes dehydrated.

A breakdown in the toilet habits of old
dogs can again often be attributed to medical
causes, and there is little that can be done,
although in cystitis (inflammation of the
bladder), appropriate medication may resolve

the problem rapidly. An adult male dog
brought into a new household can prove
troublesome by cocking its leg around the
furniture. This is not indicative of a urinary
problem, but rather that the dog is using its
urine to mark its new territory. This is
particularly likely to occur if you are
introducing a second dog alongside an existing
pet. Under these circumstances you need to
review your attitude to the dogs. Perhaps you
are ignoring your existing pet, and giving
preferential treatment to the newcomer? This
will simply serve to increase the possibility of
conflict between the two dogs, because the
social status of the newcomer is raised by your
actions. Instead, you should make a greater
fuss of the established dog, and so reinforce its
dominant position over the newcomer. (You
will find more on this subject in Chapter 4.)

Dogs which have lived in kennels for a long
time can be particularly difficult to house-train
successfully, although this is helped by the fact
that they will only defecate about twice a day.
You will then be in a position to feed your dog,
and take it out for a walk until it has relieved
itself, bearing in mind that it must be
prevented from taking strenuous exercise at
this stage. In any event, the dog may be too
nervous to allow it to run free at this stage, and
to be trusted to return to you. Give it plenty of
encouragement by allowing it to pause to sniff
the ground if it wishes. It should then pick a
suitable spot.

Alternatively, you can allow the dog out
into the garden, encouraging it to perform here
by the use of the words 'clean dog' or whatever
phrase you decide to choose to demand such
activity. Plenty of praise should be given when
the dog responds, although there is no point in
scolding it if it fails to do anything more than
run or sniff around the garden.

You should keep a close watch on a new
dog in particular in these surroundings,
because often they may try to escape from the
garden, and go wandering. Dogs are
surprisingly agile, and may leap over fences or

even burrow under them, particularly if there is a bitch on heat nearby. This is why it is essential that they should wear a collar with a name tag attached at all times.

Rescued dogs are often somewhat nervous of people, and yet may also become excited to see you, when you have been out, for example. These factors in turn give rise to the condition which is described as submissive urination. This can arise in dogs which are house-trained, and does not reflect a breakdown in the training process because it is an involuntary action on the dog's part. After greeting you frantically, the dog rolls over on to its back, and a small volume of urine is passed at the same time. This can sometimes even occur while the

dog is standing, and such behaviour tends to be more common in bitches.

There is little to be achieved by scolding a dog when this happens as this simply adds to the emotional charge linked to your reappearance. Instead, try not to make too much fuss of the dog when it rushes to greet you. By defusing the atmosphere surrounding this event you will lessen the likelihood of the problem arising in the future. As a precautionary measure, however, do not head straight into the house, but allow the dog to come out to see you. Then if some drops of urine are passed, these can be washed away more easily. These simple steps should ensure the problem's rapid disappearance.

BELOW
When they are very excited or fearful, bitches in particular will roll on to their backs, and dribbles of urine may be visible afterwards. This is not usually a sign of incontinence, but a behavioural response, known as 'submissive urination'.

RIGHT

Patience is important when
persuading a young puppy to
walk on the leash. They may turn
round to you for reassurance in
the early stages.

BELOW

Once the young dog has grown
in confidence, then it is more
likely to try to pull ahead, as
shown here. A check chain can
be particularly useful at this
stage, before a powerful dog
grows out of control.

Leash training

Although you will not be able to take your
puppy out for a walk in public places until it
has completed its course of inoculation, at
about 12 weeks old, the intervening weeks up to
this point will be useful in familiarizing the dog
with walking on a leash. This can be carried out
quite easily in the garden, especially if you have
a wall or fence with an adjacent path.

Remember that puppies tire much more
quickly than older dogs, so do not be tempted
to overdo training in these early stages, since
this will just be counter-productive. A brief
session morning and evening is usually to be
recommended, avoiding the middle of the day
in hot weather. Dogs should not be exercised
then, because there is a risk that they could
succumb to heat stroke. The short-nosed
(brachycephalic) breeds such as the bulldog
are most at risk.

It is standard practice for the dog to be
trained to walk on the left-hand side of its
owner, so start with this in mind. Remove the
collar and fit a choke chain and leash, or a
head-collar as described previously (see pages
14–15). Harnesses are another popular option
with owners of dachshunds, spreading the
point of control more widely over the body,
rather than just the neck or head. This is to be
recommended in this case because of the
susceptibility of these breeds to inter-vertebral
disc problems, which can arise in the vicinity
of the neck.

In the initial stages the puppy is likely to
pull on the leash by trying to rush ahead.
Continue walking at your own speed, pulling
slightly on the leash in order to tighten the
choke chain, accompanying this with the
command 'heel'. This should then encourage
the puppy to slow down, as the sensation of the
chain tightening will be unpleasant. Similarly,
pulling on the head-collar will also tend to slow
the dog down.

By this stage, you may already have booked into a dog training class. These are held in many towns, but as more people appreciate the need to train their dogs properly, so courses usually fill up quickly. It is advisable to make enquiries early on to be certain of obtaining a place. Once you have started the course, you may well be given specific routines to accomplish with your pet between these lessons. This can be particularly useful, because although your dog may well master these quite readily in the privacy of your garden, it will also need to perform them with your encouragement in the totally different environment of the training hall, in the company of other dogs.

Never assume because your dog does respond properly in its own environment that it will continue to do so elsewhere. This can be a dangerous fallacy. Your pet may be distracted by a scent, for example, and run off regardless of your instructions to sit. This type of reaction is inevitable at some point. To minimize the risk of any accident you should take your dog to a quiet spot, as far away from roads as possible, when you first extend the training process beyond the immediate confines of your garden.

LEFT
The steps in training your dog to walk correctly on the leash are shown here. At first, it can be helpful to speak quietly to your pet as you walk along, by way of encouragement. Again, consistency in approach is important. While the leash may be held in the right hand, the dog is invariably positioned on the left.

FAR LEFT
Always try to walk on the street with the dog up against a fence or wall. Here it will be less likely to pull across the pavement into the road.

THE COMMAND 'SIT'

RIGHT

With the dog standing still, give the command 'sit'. Gentle pressure over the hindquarters as shown may first be necessary to evoke the required response.

RIGHT

Sitting is a natural posture for dogs, and they should feel quite happy in this position.

RIGHT

You should be able to kneel down, keeping the leash held high, without upsetting your dog.

Leash training should also be linked with other basic commands which will be essential when the dog is walking along the streets. For example, it must learn to sit, rather than straining to rush across a road. You can begin this aspect of training right from the outset, encouraging the puppy to sit in advance of every meal.

Apply gentle pressure to the dog's hindquarters to encourage it to sit. This can be repeated at the start of every session of leash training: hold the leash in your right hand and then apply a light touch with your left hand. Do not allow the leash to slacken at this point, but try to keep it taut as this will help to ensure the puppy adopts the required position rather than jumping up.

If you encounter problems, you may want to kneel down alongside the dog, keeping your hand in place over the hindquarters and the leash in an upright position. Do not be too keen to give praise in this intance, but allow the dog to settle down first for a few moments. You will soon find that the dog will sit of its own accord, before you place the food bowl in front of it, as this is a natural posture for dogs to adopt.

Having started on the leash from the sitting position, you should also break the walk with the command 'sit', as will be necessary when you are opening the car door, for example, or when you come to a road. You can also encourage your dog to sit when it is playing in the garden. Such behaviour is essential when you are training your dog to run free outside as you will want to put it back on the leash at the end of the period of exercise. Sitting is a relatively straightforward command to teach, and because it is such an

important part of many other routines you should concentrate on this command during the early stages of training.

By the time your young dog is about six months old you should be developing other commands which will form part of its outdoor training requirements, in preparation for allowing the dog off its leash. These sessions should not be too long, just five minutes or so, two or three times every day. Continuity is important, and the dog is likely to respond best to one person, especially when learning new routines.

Once these routines have been mastered, then other members of the family can encourage the dog to behave in the required fashion. As an example, whoever feeds the dog should always insist that it sits before placing the bowl down on the ground. Make sure that the same commands are given, however, to prevent confusion and a likely lack of response on the dog's part. The word 'sit', for example, should be used at all times rather than simply saying 'food' in this instance, and hoping that the dog will respond accordingly.

ABOVE AND RIGHT
When you are carrying out any training procedure, especially outside, it is important to select a quiet locality. This applies especially when teaching a dog to sit, because this is quite a relaxed posture, and any distractions will upset the dog's concentration.

Staying

Concentrate on giving straightforward instructions, remembering the significance of the tone of voice. Use an encouraging, clear tone and avoid repeating the command immediately if the dog fails to respond at once. Otherwise, the repetition on your part will not motivate the dog to react at first, and soon this can become an habitual problem.

Training sessions should be fun, and the dog must be encouraged as an active participant. Once it is sitting on command, you can develop this into staying as well. This is sometimes surprisingly difficult to master, especially with more exuberant individuals, simply because they will run after you.

Start with the dog on the leash, commanding it to sit before stepping back. Repeat the word 'sit' to reinforce the dog's posture. If the dog tries to follow you wait until it has readopted a sitting posture. This can be accomplished either by placing your hand back over its hindquarters, or if this fails by using a choke chain. If the dog moves, your grip will pull the lead vertically and tighten the chain as the dog moves towards you.

Once the dog responds as required then offer plenty of encouragement. The next stage is to persuade it to remain in position while you move away, with the leash lying on the ground. This will be much harder to achieve if you start with the leash held vertically because the act of lowering it will be distracting for the dog. Instead, hold the leash so that it is close to the ground from the start, before the dog sits. Then you can simply release your grip and back slowly away over a few paces. If you move fast, then the dog is more likely to follow you. An extendable leash may be helpful at this stage. Repeating the exercise regularly will soon pay off.

RIGHT

It is important to choose a place away from roads when you are encouraging your dog to stay. Neither should there be dogs or other animals in the vicinity.

LEFT

Once the dog is sitting, you can then extend the leash on the ground. Hand signals are an important part of the trainer's repertoire, the raised hand here indicating 'stay'.

BELOW LEFT

There is no need to let your dog off the leash at first when you are teaching the 'stay' command. Here it is simply trailed on the ground to the trainer.

BELOW

Training is a sequence of lessons, and at this stage, you can move back towards the dog and slip off its leash. Always leave the collar on under these circumstances so that you can restrain the dog more easily, if it attempts to run off.

Obviously once you are in a position where the dog remains still as you move away the basics of the command have been mastered. You can either call the dog to you or else leave it sitting and return to it. Avoid confusion, however, by adopting a standard approach at first. It is probably better to return to the dog until the 'sit and stay' command is well established. Otherwise, by calling the dog, you may encourage it to simply stand up and then race across the ground.

RIGHT

This Weimaraner bitch has clearly mastered the 'sit and stay' command. Note that while the dog's body remains still, it is nonetheless alert and watchful, awaiting further instructions from its owner.

One of the major concerns about dogs is the slight yet potential danger to human health which exists from the parasitic worm called *Toxocara canis*. The risk stems from the fact that if these microscopic eggs are inadvertently swallowed by a child, then the larval stage in this parasite's life-cycle can develop in the human body. Larvae can then move from the child's intestinal tract into the tissues, this phase sometimes being described as *visceral larval migrans*. Should these larvae reach the eye, then they are likely to encyst and cause

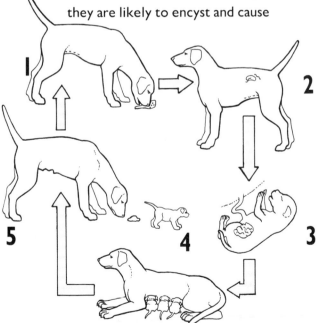

blindness. The number of actual cases recorded annually is, however, tiny.

Regular deworming will largely eliminate the risk of this infection, and to prevent puppies representing a danger, most vets recommend that they should be treated from two weeks old onwards, as well as their mothers. Apart from being spread externally, via eggs, pregnant bitches can pass the parasite directly to their puppies across the placenta before birth, and also via their milk.

Once the worms are established in the puppy's gut, they will start to produce eggs which are expelled with the faeces. These will then take several days in the environment to mature to an infective stage. After this period, however, they can remain viable for possibly years, and so heavy soil infestation is likely to build up in places where dogs congregate, such as public parks. If you have young children, therefore, you should encourage them to wash their hands thoroughly if they have touched the ground – and always before eating or drinking.

Signs of a roundworm infection in puppies are likely to be a pot-bellied appearance and poor coat condition. In older dogs, however, the symptoms are less obvious. It is often possible to identify the characteristic eggs from a faecal sample, but regular treatment against this and other similar parasites is usually deemed preferable.

The embryonated infective eggs or larvae of the dog roundworm, *Toxocara canis* are ingested by the dog (**1**) and migrate to the body tissues (**2**) such as the kidneys. Unfortunately, the larvae usually enter the tissues of developing foetuses (**3**) and localise in their intestines, being activated by the pregnancy. After the birth of the puppies the larvae can also migrate into the puppies' system and infect them through the mother's milk (**4**) The worms mature passing eggs in the puppies' faeces which are consumed by the mother and can reinfect her (**5**). Alternatively, larvae which fail to establish themselves and are passed out in the faeces, may find another host and begin producing eggs. The eggs are not immediately infective, but need a short period outside the body to mature.

Lying down

A variation of the 'sit and stay' routine is to encourage your dog to lie down, and remain in this position until called. It is usually learnt quite quickly once the initial response has been mastered. At first, though, you may well have to encourage your dog to alter its posture from a sitting to a lying position. You can do this quite simply by lifting the forelimbs together and gently pressing down on the top of the shoulders.

When the dog is lying down, stay nearby and give the command 'down'. If this is carried out after a period of exercise your dog may readily remain in this position since it may be relatively tired. Alternatively, it may simply attempt to stand up or sit. If it does, simply repeat the procedure until it is lying down. Obviously, do not expect your pet to settle down readily on a wet or uncomfortable surface. You can reinforce the message by holding the leash close to the ground which will make it harder for the dog to stand up if it

RIGHT
At the end of a training session, always remember to pat the dog, and give words of praise. Although dogs will not actually understand what you are saying, they will definitely respond to your tone of voice.

persistently tries to do so. This is possibly more effective than having to reposition the dog repeatedly in the 'down' position.

Again, as with the sit and stay command, you can gradually back away, leaving the dog lying on the ground. Having learnt this routine previously, then dogs soon adapt to the new version. It is important for a dog to sit and stay when instructed, once you allow it to run free off a leash; while it must also be prepared to lie down, both in the home and when waiting with you out of doors.

In an emergency this may prevent a dog from straying into a potentially dangerous situation, for example if you should suddenly encounter riders on horseback when you are out for a walk along a narrow path. If the dog drops down as commanded then it will be unlikely to disturb the horses, which may otherwise be unnerved and could even attempt to bolt off.

Another situation where the command 'down' is essential is within the home itself. While it may be pleasant to have a young exuberant puppy bounding out to greet you with great enthusiasm, you do not want a large adult dog behaving in a similar fashion, leaping up and bowling people onto the floor.

This again requires consistency in training from the outset. It is unfair to expect an adult dog to appreciate that such actions are no longer welcomed if you have allowed them since it was a puppy. Try to provide just a welcome pat when you return home or first thing in the morning, rather than a more exuberant greeting. If your dog does try to jump up, simply encourage it to lie down by using the technique described previously. Be calm and firm throughout so that there is no question of the dog interpreting your anger as excitement, and striving to obtain more attention by this means.

Excitable children can have a similar effect, and so they may also have to be shown how to behave towards a puppy. This applies especially with larger breeds, such as the Great

LEFT
The command 'down' is especially important for larger dogs, so that they do not cause problems in the home. From a sitting position, the dog's front legs will need to be lowered as shown here.

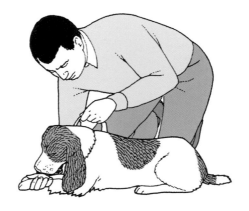

LEFT
The dog should then be reasonably comfortable. It is best to carry out this exercise in the home, or on a dry patch of grass, so that the dog can rest happily.

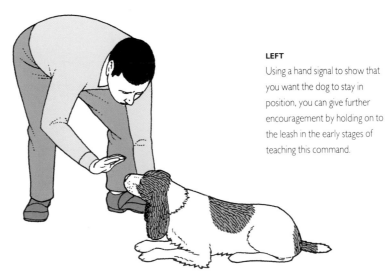

LEFT
Using a hand signal to show that you want the dog to stay in position, you can give further encouragement by holding on to the leash in the early stages of teaching this command.

RIGHT
After jumping up, this dog is being scolded for his behaviour. You should push the dog down, and give the command 'sit', before speaking to it. This will help to concentrate its attention on you.

FACING PAGE
Many dogs will instinctively jump up, either to seize a toy or as a greeting. While this may not create such serious problems if the dog is a small Jack Russell terrier, a larger dog could quite easily knock someone over and cause serious injury.

Dane, because they will grow up rapidly, and may bowl over young children. Similarly, when you have visitors, your dog must not be allowed to jump up on them. It is a good idea to let the dog remain with you, however, preferably lying down at your feet. Once this routine has been established in puppyhood you should have no difficulty with your pet when visitors call.

The only alternative is to shut your dog in a separate room when there are guests, but this could result in other problems including whining and destructive behaviour. Again, these problems are most likely to arise in puppyhood. It is usual for young puppies to whine to attract their mother's attention. This in turn becomes easily transposed onto their owner, and can become a major problem in later life.

If a dog wants food, for example when you are preparing a meal, then it may well start to whine until you give it some scraps. Unfortunately, your dog will soon come to associate its whining with an immediate and affirmative response on your part. It is therefore folly to give in to behaviour of this kind, and you should try to prevent it by being aware of the situation when it may arise and not responding as the dog demands.

Chewing behaviour

When they are teething, at between four and six months of age, puppies become especially destructive. This is the period when the milk or deciduous teeth are being shed, to be replaced by permanent adult teeth. During this stage there is a considerable increase in the number of teeth in the mouth, from 28 to 42.

You should provide suitable, safe chews, available from pet shops, to help your dog through this difficult period. You must anticipate some damage around the home at this stage, especially if you leave your pet on its own for any length of time. It is likely to be not just shoes or slippers which are chewed: the legs of a table or chair, a bed or other furniture are equally vulnerable. Take particular care not to leave live electrical flexes trailing in an exposed position or even behind a chair where the puppy could conceal itself. This could result in a fire flaring up, causing possible injury and, especially if you are out at the time, widespread damage.

It may be preferable to keep the puppy in a suitable pen while it is teething when you are away from home. This will restrict the possibility of damage being caused in your absence. Suitable designs which clip together are available especially from larger pet shops. Be sure to provide a comfortable bed, which can be a cardboard box with its sides cut down and lined with a blanket. Replace the box as necessary when it is chewed.

Encourage the puppy to recognize its own chews by handing them to it. At first the dog may only sniff at them but you should soon be able to encourage it to play with them. If not, simply leave them nearby, and the dog will probably pick them up in due course. You can buy chews which are impregnated with appealing flavours, such as ham. Although these odours are not discernible by the human nose, the highly developed scenting ability of the dog means that it can detect the flavour easily.

Try to keep as close a watch as possible on your puppy throughout the teething period. Then if you find it is starting to gnaw something which it shouldn't you can direct its attention elsewhere. Do not scold the puppy, but simply and firmly say 'no' at this stage.

Another important lesson can be begun by this stage. The young dog must learn to give up items when told to do so without attempting to snap at you. The command 'drop' is often used here. At first you may have to prize open the jaws gently, but soon the puppy should learn to release the item without hesitation, if encouraged to do so by a display of affection afterwards. Again, it is vital to state your dominance right from the start. Even a playful nip is likely to be painful and may well lead to further displays of such aggression.

RIGHT

An uncontrollable urge to chew is typical of young puppies as their set of deciduous teeth is shed, and replaced by 42 permanent ones. To divert the puppy from furniture and other household items, provide a 'chew' or toy, such as this mouse.

RIGHT

Examining your dog's mouth should be an integral part of the everyday training process. Otherwise, when this suddenly becomes necessary, the dog may actively resent it, and become aggressive. Start while the dog is still a young puppy, using the grip as shown here.

Biting

Playful biting is usual in young puppies, but this trait should have been lost by the time they are about four-and-a-half months old. Their teeth are sharp, and if you are bitten it is important to take firm action. It is preferable to smack the dog with your hand rather than use a rolled-up newspaper which the dog may see as an extension of the game, especially if it gets excited and a tug-of-war ensues. A tap over the hindquarters, accompanied by a harsh 'no'

should be adequate. Then ignore the puppy entirely for a few minutes, emphasizing that no further play will follow under these circumstances.

A better alternative to a smack is a quick squirt from a water-pistol if the dog tries to persist in this antisocial behaviour. It confirms your rejection, giving the dog an unpleasant sensation without using your hands. There is otherwise a risk that the dog may become somewhat fearful of your hands, which is obviously not to be recommended. The more

LEFT
Firm action needs to be taken towards a young dog which tries to bite, although during the teething phase, it is not unusual for many dogs to attempt to bite at their owner's hand. Their attention should be directed elsewhere, to a suitable chew.

dominant breeds such as the Dobermann must be firmly trained from puppyhood since there is otherwise a real risk that they will become aggressive in later life.

In some cases aggression can be traced back to incidents which happened in the puppy's past. Never take the dog's food away if you discover that it has misbehaved, or if it refuses to sit. This will simply make the dog hungry and it will exert its possessiveness towards the food by snarling if you try to approach. You can help to prevent any problem at this time simply by not giving the dog all its food in the bowl at once. Instead, you can add some more to it so the dog will not feel threatened by your presence nearby, and indeed will come to welcome it. The actual quantity of food provided in this way is not significant, although, of course, you should not overfeed for fear of making your dog obese

It is not a good idea to allow young children to feed a dog without adult supervision, and never leave them alone together. A child's curious nature, coupled with their relative lack of fear, mean that they will be vulnerable and may end up being badly injured as a consequence.

Wait until the dog has finished licking out the food bowl before removing it. The greatest risk of conflict is at mealtimes. By bringing up a puppy in the context of a set routine, the anxiety factor present in dogs (and humans alike) will not be brought into play and so lead to an aggressive outburst.

In the past, fleas used to be a problem only during the warmer months of the year in temperate areas, but now the advent of central heating has enabled these parasites to plague dogs and their owners for much of the year. The presence of fleas on your dog does not indicate neglect, as the cleanest of dogs can be host to these parasites, which feed on blood. Adult fleas are equipped with sharp, piercing mouthparts to penetrate the dog's skin.

You may well notice at first that your dog scratches persistently when it is infected, in spite of being told to stop doing so. Regular grooming with a special fine flea comb should alert you to the presence of these troublesome parasites. Look for tiny specks of black dirt – these are the flea droppings.

If you are in doubt about these, sprinkle the debris from the comb on to a piece of white paper, and pour a little water over it. The dark specks will dissolve, producing a reddish-brown coloration on the paper, because of traces of undigested blood in the flea dirt. Actual fleas themselves may be harder to locate, although the base of the tail is a good point to look for them. One of the advantages of grooming your dog outside is that if any do leap off at this stage, then they are not likely to cause problems in the home.

Fleas can be treated by means of either a powder or spray, or by giving your dog a medicated bath. It is also important not to forget any cats in the household, as fleas can spread back and forth between dogs and cats, although not all canine treatments are suitable for cats. In addition, if you are treating your pets outside, avoid using a spray near a pond, as this may be toxic for fish. The same applies indoors, if you have an aquarium. Here, you must also treat the dog's bed and bedding, and possibly the carpet, because fleas breed off the dog in its environment.

On occasion, in the case of a severe explosion in the numbers of fleas, you may need to take more radical action to eliminate them. Pest control companies can undertake this task for you, with minimum disturbance.

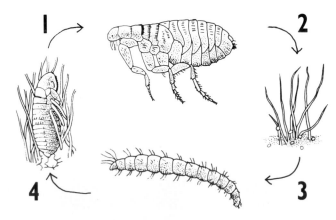

The female dog flea (**1**) lays her eggs on the floor (**2**) or in bedding and in about a week they hatch into larvae (**3**) which spin cocoons, inside which the pupae (**4**) develop into adults within two or three weeks.

The dog flea acts as an intermediate host for the larvae of the common tapeworm, *Dipylium caninum* which makes it even more vital that flea infestations should be controlled.

Behaviour in the home

You will need to integrate the new puppy into socializing with people outside your immediate family. Some of these guests may not like dogs, and could be nervous, especially if you have a large breed. This can cause complications since the dog will undoubtedly be able to sense this

by jumping up at a visitor while they are sitting down. Although this may seem quite appealing behaviour in a young puppy, it will be seen in a totally different light with a large adult Irish Wolfhound. Again, consistency when training is important, and it is generally better not to allow dogs on to furniture. Otherwise, cleaning the room inevitably becomes more difficult as

LEFT
Never forget that small puppies can grow into large dogs, as shown by this Pyrenean Mountain dog. There is little space left to sit down here, while the dribbling habits of some dogs will not improve your sofa's condition. You may prefer to discourage your dog from sleeping on the furniture, even while it is a puppy.

fear, and may respond aggressively. At first you may well have to put the puppy on its leash and keep it close to you if it is not to be an annoyance when visitors call. Obviously the puppy will be curious and should be allowed to meet your guests. However, it should not be allowed to continue making a nuisance of itself

hairs are shed over the chair covers, and there is an increased risk of flea infestations.

These troublesome parasites, which now thrive throughout the year in centrally-heated homes provided that the humidity level is not too low, can bite people as well as dogs and cats. The crevices at the sides of chairs provide

Instead, provide a suitable bed in a corner of the room. It is important to teach your dog to return here when required. After an initial greeting of a visitor, tell your dog to sit in its bed using the command 'bed'.

There are several ways of accomplishing this, and it is of the greatest importance that you teach the puppy to recognize its bed. This can be carried out last thing at night, once the puppy has been outside to relieve itself. By this stage it will be ready to sleep, and you should give the word 'bed' at this time, placing the puppy back in its bed if necessary.

Once the puppy is properly toilet trained it may be more convenient to move the bed out of the kitchen into another room in the house. Your dog will still identify with its bed in a new location, especially if a piece of familiar bedding is provided. Once the teething phase has passed you may want to get a new bed, rather than a cardboard box with its sides cut down. Wicker beds may look attractive, but can be difficult to clean properly, which will be necessary from time to time, especially if your dog suffers from fleas. A solid plastic bed is

ABOVE
Bean bags of various types are now used widely for dogs. They are ideal for large breeds, or individuals which have a back ailment of any kind and may find it painful to curl up in a basket.

an ideal refuge for fleas at all stages in their lifecycle. Since fleas do jump, of course, there is no certainty that they will not occasionally land on a chair, but the likelihood is greatly reduced if the dog is kept off furniture.

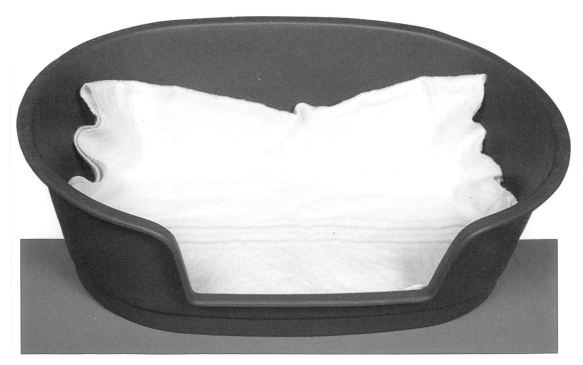

RIGHT
This type of bed is easily cleaned – an important consideration to prevent the build-up of fleas in the dog's environment. The lining is disposable, although alternatively, you could use a blanket.

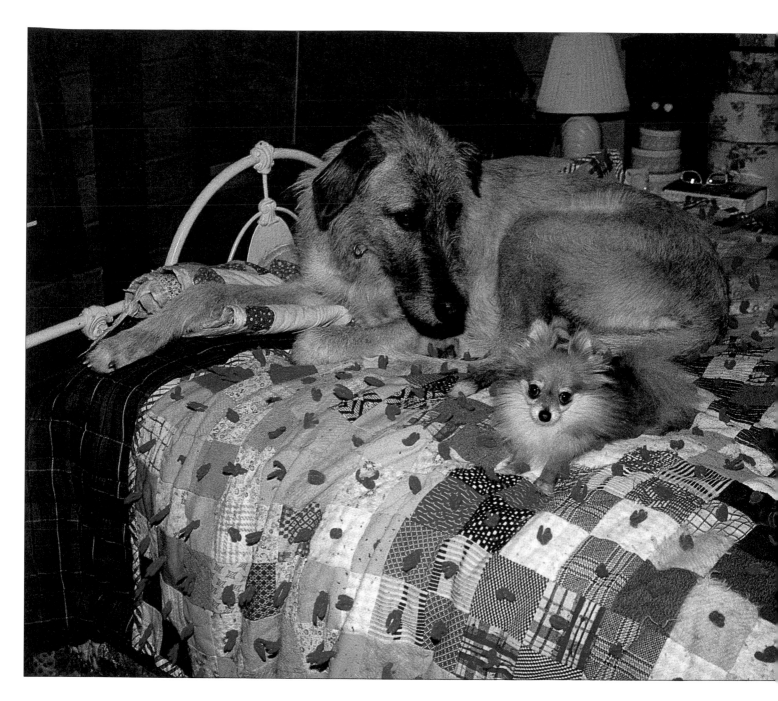

much more satisfactory for this purpose, provided that it will not be chewed.

If you wish to keep the dog's bed outside your sitting room, in the kitchen for example, you can still provide a bean bag so there will be no need for your dog to climb on the furniture. Choose a brand with a removable outer cover, so this can be washed easily, while, as a precaution, the contents should be fire-retardant. Your dog can be trained to stay or sleep here while you are talking to visitors in the room or, indeed, sitting there on your own.

A dog will not be deprived if it cannot use a chair. As creatures of habit, you will find that they soon do not even attempt to climb on furniture, but voluntarily retire to their bed. Try to place this in a quiet corner of the room away from the door, especially if you have young children. The puppy can then be left alone to sleep with relatively little disturbance.

ABOVE

Dogs large and small will frequent the bedroom if they have an opportunity, but this should be discouraged. You may otherwise find yourself being badly bitten by fleas.

THREE
THE ADULT DOG

THE ADULT DOG

The puppyhood phase is essentially over by the time the young dog is six months old. Now is a good time to review training progress. All the basic lessons should now have been mastered, at least within the confines of a garden. The dog will respond readily to its name, and will recognize other members of the family. With regard to other pets, puppies generally learn at an early stage not to pursue a cat sharing the home with them. If you notice any difficulty in this respect, catch the puppy and utter a firm 'no'

In most instances the cat will tend to be the dominant animal and may occasionally resort to scratching the dog if it proves a nuisance. Most dogs will then rapidly modify their behavioural response to cats in general, and no further conflicts result. In some cases cats actively seek the company of dogs living alongside them and a more harmonious relationship can develop under these circumstances.

In the outdoor environment, the dog will be used to walking on the leash with you. It should follow the command 'heel' without difficulty, and will also sit at the side of a road before being told to cross. Dogs are curious, inquisitive animals by nature, however, and so may sometimes be wayward. A scent on a tree

RIGHT
Although dogs will often live peacefully with cats, you should not trust them with smaller pets such as rabbits, which are the natural quarry of many hounds.

stump or lamp-post may distract a dog which happily walks to heel around the garden.

It will be a matter of striking a balance between allowing your dog to pause constantly along a path, sniffing at every opportunity, and walking with no chance to explore its environment. Generally in towns where there are pavements, dogs should be expected to walk properly. If they stop and pause they may well urinate or even defecate at that spot, which is likely to be not only illegal, but also certainly socially undesirable. In a large park, however, well away from any paths and children's play areas, it will not be so serious if your dog relieves itself.

As a responsible dog owner you must be prepared to deworm your dog regularly, not only for the sake of its health and other dogs, but also to protect people from the risk of the disease toxocariasis, as mentioned previously (see page 36) From six months onwards, deworming will probably be required about twice a year on average. Treatment for tapeworms can also start at this age. This group of parasites tend not to be such a problem in young dogs as roundworms. However, one particular type, called *Dipylidium caninum*, is spread by fleas. It is therefore vital to control fleas if you are to prevent infection by this species of tapeworm.

LEFT
Once the basic lessons have been mastered with the dog on its leash, you should then repeat them without this restraint. This retriever is walking to heel.

RIGHT
The value of having taught the dog to allow you to open its mouth is clearly visible here. Fluid medication should be given in the side of the mouth, rather than at the front. From this position it is less likely to run out over the fur.

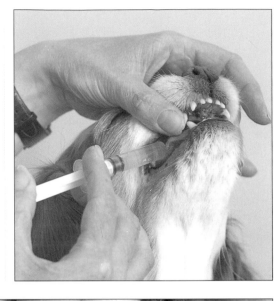

BELOW
When administering tablets, do not break them, as many have an unpleasant taste.

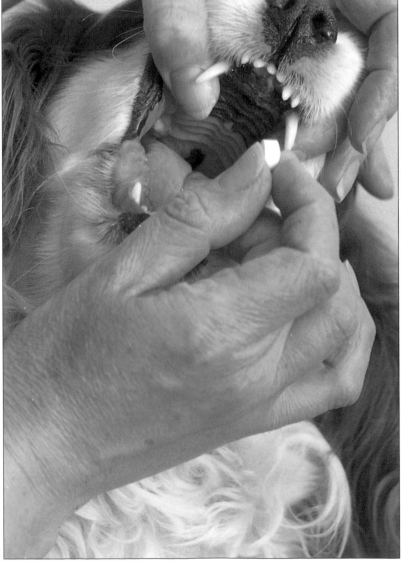

Veterinary training

When you are giving tablets to your dog, it may be possible simply to disguise them in food, such as a piece of meat, which can then be added to the dog's meal. You must check that the tablet is actually consumed, rather than simply being left in the bottom of the bowl. Should this method fail, then you are likely to be forced to place the tablet directly into its mouth. Do not attempt to break up the tablet instead and powder it over the food at the next meal. This is because some tablets, especially those prescribed for deworming purposes, often have a nasty taste and may cause your dog to salivate if they are swallowed in this form. Normally, the drug itself is retained by a protective coating which conceals its taste.

If you need to give a tablet directly to your dog, it may be helpful to have someone else to assist you by holding the dog. It is reasonably easy to open the dog's mouth by putting your left hand on either side of the upper jaw, while prizing the lower jaw apart with your other hand. (Obviously you will find it easier to reverse the positioning of your hands if you are left-handed.)

Holding the tablet with the thumb and first finger of your right hand, drop this as far back as possible in the dog's mouth, without releasing your grip on the jaws. You must then close the mouth, so as to encourage the dog to swallow the tablet. It will help to tilt the head slightly upwards, and stroke the throat area at the same time.

As a routine measure, you should open your dog's mouth each week, so that it becomes used to this procedure. Dogs may otherwise prove rather snappy under these circumstances. This is not only important for giving tablets, but it also enables you to inspect their teeth. A number of dental care products, including special canine toothbrushes and paste are now available, and it is advisable to use these regularly. This will help to prevent the build-up of harmful plaque on the teeth, especially close to the border with the gums. Here it is particularly harmful, as it is likely to trigger inflammation known as gingivitis, which can result in erosion of the gum and weakening of the teeth. In addition, a build-up of plaque is a common cause of bad breath, known technically as halitosis, which is unpleasant and easily prevented in this case.

A third reason for being able to open your dog's mouth easily is if it swallows a bone, or a ball becomes stuck here. In such emergency situations your dog will be frightened anyway, and you will need to protect yourself as far as possible against being bitten. This will be almost inevitable if the dog is not used to having its mouth opened. Yet if it is not

alarmed by this procedure, you may well be able to relieve the obstruction and so prevent the dog from choking at a time when rapid action is required.

A slightly different procedure is required if you need to give your dog a liquid medicine using a syringe, and, again, you can practise this slightly different grip. In this instance, the jaws should be held together with the nose pointing upwards. The tip of the syringe is then inserted from the side of the mouth, and the plunger gently depressed so as not to cause the medication to run out of the mouth. Never attempt to pour liquid medication straight into the mouth from the front or spoon it in, since this will inevitably cause choking.

LEFT
Brushing your dog's teeth will guard against bad breath. Once used to this procedure, your dog will not be worried by it – but take care not to hurt the gums, which are quite sensitive.

It is important to bear in mind that a dog will not forget an unhappy experience of this nature, and almost certainly, at some stage in its life, it will require treatment which has to be given orally. You may then find yourself faced with a real battle if your dog has not been taught to co-operate in this fashion. It can make all the difference to a successful outcome to a course of medication, yet, unfortunately, the majority of dog owners rarely consider this aspect of training.

Similarly, you should not just look at the eyes or ears when there may be a problem here. You may want to wipe around the eyes with moist cotton wool on occasions as part of the regular grooming process, and also inspect the ears. You can use a cotton wool bud to remove any obvious build-up of dirt in the ear canal, but never be tempted to probe here, as this may cause injury.

Ear infections are most likely to occur in breeds with relatively long and heavy ears, such as spaniels. Again, apart from alerting you to the likely development of a problem here, such inspections will help to ensure that even with a painful condition, the dog will have sufficient confidence to allow you to treat it without attempting to snap or simply pulling its head away repeatedly.

It is especially important in these cases to apply the medication effectively in order to cure the condition. Recurrences are otherwise quite likely, and, ultimately, surgery may be the only recourse. You can help when providing the medication by massaging the side of the ear. Take care to be gentle, since these ear infections are intensely irritating and painful.

Another useful training procedure for health purposes is to lift the dog's feet regularly so that you can examine them. This will reveal any overgrowth of the claws, which will have to be trimmed back. You can do this yourself, although it will probably be better if you arrange for a vet to undertake the task in the first instance, as it is important to judge the required length properly. If the nail is cut too short then it will almost inevitably bleed.

Being able to examine the feet easily is also important if the dog becomes lame at any stage. It may be that a grass seed has

penetrated between the paws. This is a very painful condition, and there is a risk that the seed responsible may track further up the leg. Yet if you can see it still protruding, you can retrieve it before serious harm is caused.

Harvest mites (*Trombicula autumnalis*) may cause severe irritation between the toes during the late summer in particular, and result in the dog chewing fiercely at its feet. Treatment in this instance is likely to require the bathing of the region with a safe insecticide. This will be much easier to do if the dog will allow you to lift its feet. You will then be able to soak them in the medicated solution for maximum effectiveness.

Paw injuries are sadly not uncommon, especially on sharp pieces of glass which can inflict a nasty cut. In spite of their horny appearance, a dog's pads will bleed profusely if cut. Efficient emergency treatment relies upon being able to stem the blood loss with a tourniquet around the foot. You will find this task so much easier if the dog is used to the routine of having its leg lifted. You can then concentrate much more effectively on dealing with the wound, rather than having to battle with your dog in order to help it.

Regrettably, few owners of pet dogs consider such manoeuvres to be part of the regular training routine and yet they can be so vital in preventing the dog from becoming unnecessarily upset when it is injured.

ABOVE
The eyes of some breeds, such as Setters and Poodles, may need to be wiped quite regularly to remove accumulations of tear fluids, which can otherwise stain the fur and look unpleasant.

ABOVE, RIGHT

Regular cleaning of the upper part of the ear is recommended, and may help to prevent infections from becoming established lower down in the ear canal. These can prove very painful, as well as being difficult to get rid of – recurrences are not uncommon.

ABOVE, LEFT

If you decide to clip your dog's nails, be sure not to cut them too short. Otherwise this will cause quite severe pain and bleeding.

LEFT

Practising bandaging your pet's foot can help to prepare for the real event. Cut pads, often sliced on discarded glass in undergrowth, are sadly all too common.

LEFT

(1) Grooming needs to be carried out regularly to prevent your dog's coat from becoming matted. It will remove dead hair, and may also reveal signs of fleas.

(2) A brush will be essential for the first stage in the process. After this, you can use a comb, having hopefully removed most tangles by brushing.

(3) Use the brush in accordance with the natural contours of the dog's fur. This will depend to some extent on the breed concerned. It is usual to brush the body first, before proceeding to the legs.

(4) Take particular care when you are grooming in the vicinity of the dog's neck and head, being sure not to pull any tangles. These should instead be prised apart with your fingers.

(5) Ideally, you should brush the dog at a convenient height for you. While small dogs can be lifted quite easily on a table, this is likely to prove harder with larger individuals. In any event, it is important that the dog stands still while it is being groomed. You may need to provide a mat on a slippery surface.

(6) Regular coat care will enable your dog to look its best, and serves to emphasize the distinctive features of many breeds, such as this Pomeranian.

Grooming and bathing

Some dogs obviously require more grooming than others, and a variety of tools are available for this purpose, ranging from combs and brushes to scissors and clippers. It is important to train your dog to accept grooming as part of its regular routine. Indeed, if neglected, a dog's coat may become so tangled and matted that the poor creature will have to be anaesthetized in order to restore its coat to a good condition.

An unkempt coat will provide a refuge for parasites, and if soiled with faecal matter is likely to attract flies. These may then lay their eggs here, with the resulting maggots actually attacking the dog's skin. This condition, described as 'fly strike', can prove fatal, since the maggots liberate toxins into the blood stream, as well as permitting infection of the bodily tissues.

Daily grooming is to be recommended for most breeds, and it can be helpful to allow a puppy to become used to the sensation, even though its coat will probably need less attention than that of an adult dog.

In most cases it will be easier to groom the dog on a table, as this saves having to bend down. Make sure that the surface is comfortable and not slippery. At first, the dog may be reluctant to stay put, so restrain it by the collar. Again, it is surprising that some people never familiarize their dogs with the sensation of being picked up. In the case of a particularly large breed this is perhaps understandable, because of the sheer weight. In the case of a puppy, it is reasonably straightforward, using the hands to hold the body between the forelegs, and supporting the hindquarters on an arm. With a larger dog, however, place one arm around the hindquarters with the other encircling the forelimbs. It may be helpful to bend down to do this so as to minimize the strain on your back, especially with a heavy dog.

You will probably not have to lift your dog up frequently, but it is important that it

RIGHT
Professional grooming expertise is available, and this may be recommended if you are about to enter a show. However, much of the enjoyment of success comes from carrying out the preparatory work yourself.

BELOW
After weaning, it is never too early to introduce a dog to the sensation of being groomed. The coats of many puppies may be less profuse than that of adults, and so grooming will be more straightforward.

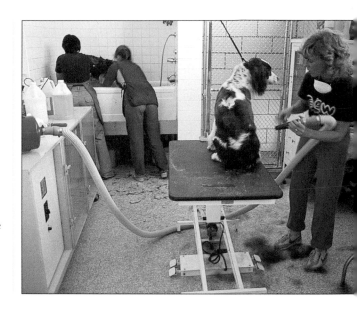

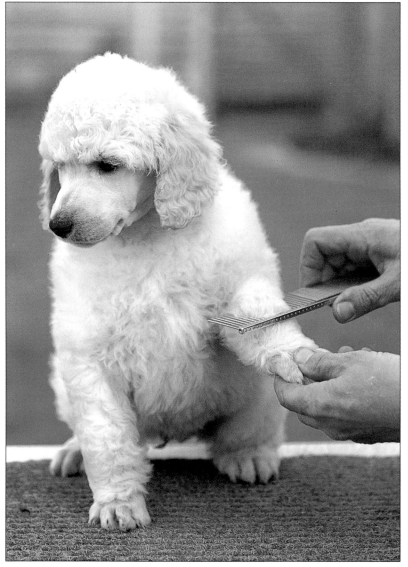

becomes used to this experience. Then, provided you have supported its body adequately, it will not try to struggle under these circumstances. There can be emergency situations, for instance if your dog cuts its paw or is bitten by a poisonous snake, when you will need to carry it back to the vehicle or home. Routinely, you are most likely to need to lift the dog up into your car, however, rather than encouraging it to jump up and possibly injure itself as a result.

From time to time it will be necessary to wash your dog's coat. This is best done outside on a warm day, using a tub or baby's bath, rather than in the bathroom itself. Apart from the problem of water being splashed all over the place, the dog may scratch the bath with its claws. It is also unhygienic, and so separate bathing facilities should be provided.

Your dog may be rather nervous of being washed and will need to be trained accordingly, especially if it is to have a career in the show ring, where careful preparation is so vital. One of the major problems is that the dog feels insecure in the water because it cannot maintain its grip properly on the base of the bath. It slides about, and slips under the water. A bad experience of this type will be enough to scare a dog for life. Sticking a rubber bath mat to the bottom of the bath from the start should help to prevent this type of reaction, and you can then lift the dog in carefully.

LEFT

For hygiene reasons, the family tub is not the best place to wash your pet. In any event, ensure that your dog's bath comes equipped with a rubber mat in the bottom, as here. Otherwise, the dog will have trouble standing up and become alarmed.

RIGHT

Always wash the dog's coat first, before the head. If you use a shower attachment rather than a simple measuring jug, take care to ensure that the water coming out of the nozzle does not suddenly change temperature.

There is no need to fill the bath to the top. As a guide, sufficient water to submerge most of the dog's legs will be adequate. This will not induce it to panic. You should always test the temperature of the water to make sure that it is neither too hot nor too cold before putting the dog in. A tepid bath is to be preferred.

When you are giving a dog a bath for the first time, it may be helpful to have someone else to help you. They can hold the dog, as it is likely to try to leap out of the bath. You will need a measuring jug, shampoo and towels on hand. Choose a special canine shampoo, and use this in accordance with the instructions, especially if it is medicated and active against parasites such as fleas, for example.

Never start by pouring water over the dog's head. Instead, using the measuring jug, bale the water gently over its back so that this runs down the sides of the body, which will be less alarming. While at first your dog may be nervous, quiet words of encouragement should help to overcome its fears. Clean all over the body before carefully shampooing the head, taking care to avoid the eyes. You may prefer to use a flannel to clean this area, as this will afford greater control.

In order to wash the shampoo out of the coat, you may prefer to lift the dog out of the bath and rinse the coat separately. Alternatively, you will need to empty the bath and refill it with clean water. Whenever you take the dog out of the bath, however, it is advisable to stand back, because invariably the dog will shake itself to remove water from its coat. You can then use a towel to dry the dog as much as possible, making sure that it does not become chilled and start shivering.

If you choose to use a hair-dryer, allow the dog to become used to the noise at close quarters. You may well find that it is scared of this unfamiliar sensation at first. Take care not to make the air jet too warm either, as this will be uncomfortable for your pet. As in many of the less obvious aspects of dog training, care over details such as this will help to ensure that there is no adverse reaction on the part of the dog. It is much better to attempt to prevent fears arising, rather than having to rectify them at a later stage.

ABOVE
Young dogs, especially those with a show career in front of them, need to become accustomed to regular bathing and drying. Persuading them to sit still can be difficult at first.

BELOW
A hair-dryer can be of great value in drying your dog's coat, while the jets of air, in conjunction with a brush, may also help to undo any tangles after a bath.

ABOVE

If you have a hatchback with collapsible rear seats, then it is easy to fit an appropriate travelling cage for your dog – thereby preventing damage to the upholstery.

LEFT

It is better to transport dogs individually, and partitioned travelling cages can be acquired for this purpose. A rug or old blanket should be placed in the cage, so that the dogs can lie down in comfort.

Car travel

Once they are used to travelling in the car, most dogs seem to enjoy being taken out in this way. At first, however, being unused to the sensations of the journey, they may well be car sick. There is little that can be done at this stage. To minimize the risk, keep the dog securely confined in a suitable travelling cage. This can be positioned in the rear of the car, but never be tempted to put a dog in a cage in the boot (trunk) of a car. It is likely to be frightened in the dark, and there is always the possibility of exhaust fumes leaking into this compartment, sometimes with deadly effects.

Always line the travelling cage with a good layer of absorbent paper, with a piece of towelling on top. Here, after a while, the dog should curl up and sleep. Try to ensure that it has relieved itself before the journey, and do not feed the dog immediately before setting out, since this appears to increase the risk of travel sickness. At first young dogs may paw at the floor and whine when confined in this way, but obviously you must ignore this while you are driving. Never allow a young dog in particular to have free access in a car, because inevitably it will prove a distraction and may even cause an accident.

It is a good idea to take a young dog out for short drives before it has completed its course of inoculations. This will help as part of the socialization process, but do bear in mind that you will not be able to allow it to scamper about at the end of the journey until you return home, because it will not be fully protected at this stage.

Most dogs are keen to travel in a car, but a bad experience can dent their enthusiasm in this respect. If your dog does start retching, do not scold it, since it will be unable to help this involuntary reaction. Instead, try to pull over if possible and find somewhere to take the dog out of the car, in its travelling cage, so that it can have fresh air. Recovery from the effects of travel sickness is very rapid. While you are

moving, make sure that the interior of the car is well ventilated, although, obviously, the dog must not be left in a direct draught.

On occasions, especially if they have been sick repeatedly, some dogs may be reluctant to enter a car. This can become a real problem unless the situation is handled cautiously, because simply lifting the dog up and placing it in the car will be counter-productive. A step-by-step approach is required: first to entice the dog into the car, then allow it to become used to resting here without being driven off. It will be ideal if you can park the car in such a way that the dog can move in and out as it wants, with the door left open, although clearly this will not be possible unless you have a driveway with a gate at the end.

BELOW
It is a bad idea to encourage a dog to jump into a vehicle as shown here. Small breeds like Dachshunds are liable to injure their backs, sometimes seriously, as a result. They should be lifted up.

The next stage will be to train the dog to sit in the car with the doors closed, and the engine turning over with you in the driver's seat. It is generally older dogs that are nervous of vehicles, especially if they are strays whose only previous experience of travelling in this fashion is being dumped in the dog warden's van.

Your car will need to be equipped with a proper dog guard if at all possible, to prevent the dog from jumping back and forth across the seats. This is particularly likely in the case of a nervous individual. For smaller breeds, a dog travelling cage may be useful. You can also buy special seat belts for dogs, to restrain their movements within a car. Adult dogs sometimes find these rather distressing, however, simply because the dog has little freedom of movement and may start to panic under these circumstances.

Dogs must be trained to behave properly in cars, however they are transported. While there is nothing to be gained by scolding an individual being sick, you should take action to prevent whining or barking, giving a firm 'no' by way of command. Should this persist with a dog housed in a travelling cage, then you can cover the cage using a blanket or sheet. The dog will then usually be quiet, and after a short period you can remove the cover. After a time, realizing that it will be deprived from human company, it should desist.

Some dogs may become over excited when taken out in the car, associating this with walks. They bark and jump around excitedly, becoming particularly frenetic if you stop somewhere else, rather than taking them immediately for a walk. By the time this stage has been reached it is rather late to try and prevent it. For this reason you should take young dogs out on various journeys, and not just when they are going for a walk. This should prevent a problem of this type from recurring.

If you have a dog that behaves in this fashion, do not encourage it by making soothing noises, entreating it to calm down. This is merely likely to reinforce this response to travelling. Instead, stop the car at a suitable spot and walk away out of sight for a few minutes. Deprived of attention, the dog should then quieten down quite quickly, and ultimately behaviour of this kind can be overcome if you then return home without allowing the dog out of the vehicle on this occasion.

You must always be careful, however, when leaving a dog in a car, that it will not succumb to heat stroke. This is not only a problem in the warmer parts of the world. In temperate climates as well many dogs die in tragic circumstances for this reason each summer. The temperature within a car with its windows closed can rise rapidly to fatal levels, literally in minutes, especially if it is parked in direct sunshine. Do not rely on ventilator grilles which can be fitted partially over a window, as these may prove inadequate.

Indeed, you should never have a window half open and leave the dog inside, effectively guarding the car. This can be disastrous, especially if young children are passing and try to make a fuss of the dog. Seeing the car as its territory, the dog may attempt to snap fiercely at them. If your dog shows signs of behaving in this fashion then you will need to train it to ignore people who come close to the car. A firm 'no' and the command 'sit' should be used for this purpose.

Another reason for keeping the dog safely confined behind a grille is to prevent damage to the upholstery of the vehicle, as could otherwise happen in your absence.

If it becomes bored, a young dog especially may try to gnaw at a seat and cause a lot of damage. In any event, it will be worthwhile fitting protective covers if the dog is allowed into the passenger seats of the vehicle at any stage, because otherwise, its hairs will stick to the upholstery.

If you find that your dog still appears distressed, in spite of all your attempts to settle it down to travel readily in a car, then you may want to speak with your vet about the problem. It might be possible to resolve the situation with a course of tranquillisers. Usually given in tablet form before a journey, a sedative of this kind may occasionally be valuable for a highly nervous dog. Once the sedative begins to take effect the dog may relax sufficiently to appreciate that the journey poses no threat, and in the future medication will be unnecessary. Relying on drugs for this purpose should be seen very much as the last resort, however, and the huge majority of dogs adapt to this form of transportation without difficulty, from an early age.

ABOVE

Ventilation is vital for dogs travelling in cars, but do make sure that they are not exposed to a powerful draught which could affect their eyes. This is another reason for travelling with the dog adequately restrained, rather than allowing it to put its head out of the window, like this Newfoundland.

LEFT
When the dog pulls ahead while on the leash, the choke chain tightens and it will experience discomfort. It will soon learn to walk at the right pace.

Within the confines of the garden your dog will have learnt the basic commands such as walking to heel and sitting. You can put these into practice when you take the dog out on to the street. Do not expect too much in the early stages, even if your dog has become a model pupil at home. There will inevitably be scents and other distractions, including passing vehicles, which will affect the dog's concentration on your commands.

For this reason, start by choosing a relatively quiet environment rather than a busy road. Be certain to keep the dog positioned on your left-hand side, away from the road at all times. If you walk reasonably close to the left side of the path there will probably be a natural barrier, such as a fence or wall, to reinforce the dog's previous training routine. You may well find that you have to use the choke chain more than normal when you are first walking along the street as the dog will be more inclined to pause for scents than before.

RIGHT
This is the ideal position for the dog to walk in. Here the choke chain is relaxed. Note that the leash itself is held in your right hand.

RIGHT
Sometimes, often because of a scent, the dog will attempt to stop while you are walking. Similarly the choke chain will again tighten, encouraging your pet to walk alongside you.

Contact with other dogs may be a problem at first as well. Try to keep your dog walking in a straight line, so that it does not pull across you to reach another dog, because otherwise you might trip over the leash. Again, if your dog seems keen to linger, give a gentle pull on the choke chain, with the command 'on', to indicate that the dog is to continue walking.

If you regularly visit shops in your neighbourhood where dogs are prohibited, it is a good idea to accustom your pet to waiting for you tied to a dog park. Never be tempted to leave the dog off the leash, hoping that it will simply sit until you emerge from the shop. A distraction may cause it to wander off into the road, with fatal consequences.

You should also make sure that the leash is tied firmly in place, so that the dog will not be able to wriggle free and disappear in your absence. Give the commands 'sit and stay' before leaving the dog, and check that it has remained in position before entering the shop. Again, plenty of praise at this stage will help to reinforce the desired response.

Never be tempted to run across a road if you are walking a dog. Your pet may be slow in responding, and this could easily result in a serious accident. Instead, cross at lights whenever possible or at a clear stretch of road where there is good visibility, rather than at a corner. While you are waiting to cross, encourage the dog to sit at the kerb, and never allow it to wander out into the road on its own.

LEFT
Here a dog is walking properly down the street. Note that in this position, it is being kept well away from the usual canine distractions, such as lampposts and trees.

LEFT
That dogs can be trained to walk on the leash with safety uppermost is shown by this guide dog helping its owner through slippery and snowy territory.

Public transport

You may actually encounter more problems when using public transport, simply because you have less control over events. If your dog is desperate to relieve itself while you are on a train journey, for example, and starts to whine, then it is difficult to deal with this situation. For this reason it is absolutely vital before setting out on a journey of this type, to plan as far as possible for this eventuality.

Your dog is likely to be nervous under these circumstances, being surrounded by people and loud, sometimes unexpected noises. Encourage the dog to remain close to you, away from the public thoroughfare as far as possible. Your dog can then watch events without fear of being trodden on and hurt by passers-by. When the bus or train arrives, lift the dog on and, if possible, carry it to your seat. This saves time and you won't block up the aisle when there are other passengers.

If you make journeys of this type regularly, then the dog will soon become used to the routine, although it is probably best not to travel with your dog on public transport if it can

be avoided. You may find that older dogs are nervous under these circumstances, if they have never been on a train or bus before, and you should always try to reassure them with your tone of voice. Offer words of encouragement and do not simply ignore the dog.

Barking

Some breeds such as Cocker Spaniels will bark repeatedly, and studies have revealed that this behaviour is far more common in dogs than in their ancestor, the grey wolf. This is perhaps not surprising since from the earliest stages of domestication, dogs have been kept for guarding purposes. A bark alerts their owner to a likely disturbance, enabling them to take effective action.

Today's breeds have been largely developed with this trait in mind, with the notable exception of the Basenji which, rather misleadingly, is sometimes described as the barkless dog, although it does have a reasonably extensive vocal range. Evolved for

RIGHT
The Basenji is an unusual dog in several respects, mainly because it is much quieter than other breeds. It also eats grass and benefits from a regular supply of green vegetables in its diet.

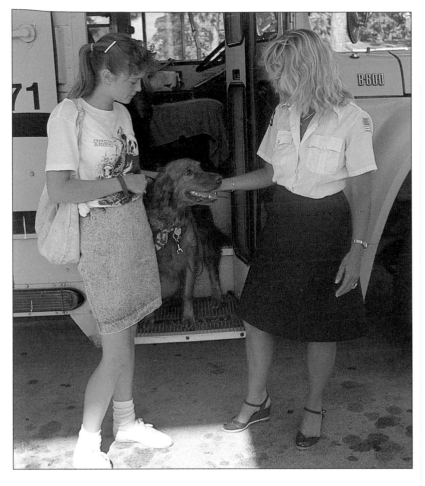

ABOVE
Dogs will soon become used to travelling on public transport, but try to avoid peak-time travel at first, as they are more likely to be accidentally hurt by other passengers.

RIGHT
Wolves live in packs, and howling serves to keep pack members in touch with each other, as well as alerting other packs to their presence. Here, in similar territory, a Siberian Husky howls to attract attention from its owner.

hunting in Africa, the quiet nature of this breed was essential so as not to alert game to the presence of dogs and hunters nearby.

The size of the dog is not necessarily an accurate reflection of its barking abilities. Some small breeds such as the Dachshunds have a relatively deep and loud bark.

In today's domestic environment, persistent barking by a dog is a frequent cause of complaint. The problem in such cases can often be traced back to the actions of the owner. Instead of allowing the dog to bark just when a doorbell rings, for instance, such behaviour is tolerated throughout the day and at night, whenever the dog demands attention. It soon comes to realize that to receive human company, barking for a bit should be sufficient. Then, by way of habit, if you leave the dog alone it will continue barking, and this noise may carry over a considerable distance.

You need to train the dog to desist from barking excessively. This is best achieved from an early age, by telling it to be 'quiet' once you are aware, say, that the front doorbell has

been rung. If the dog continues, then place it in another room on its own, re-emphasizing the word 'quiet'. The dog may start to scratch at the door to be let out. Further action will probably be necessary to prevent damage to the door. A firm tap on the hindquarters, accompanied by 'no' and 'bed' if appropriate, depending on the room, should put a stop to this destructive behaviour before it becomes a serious problem. Only when the dog has stopped barking should you allow it to come out to join you.

Other typical situations where barking can be a problem are when a dog wants to come indoors or resents being left in a car on its own. Similar action should be taken, so that the dog is told to be quiet, and you disappear until it has stopped barking for a few moments. Try not to respond the moment it ceases as this suggests to the dog that it can get its own way by behaving in this fashion.

Special collars which give a small yet painful electric shock to deter barking are permitted to be sold in some countries, but really have no part in training a dog properly. There is a particular problem associated with

some designs in that they are activated simply by the sound of barking. They do not distinguish between individual dogs, and so the sound of a neighbour's dog may cause yours to receive a punishment shock when it has not actually been barking. Clearly, this is not a desirable state of affairs, and apart from being unfair, will also prove upsetting to your dog.

Desperate owners sometimes ask their vet if it is possible to prevent a dog barking by surgical means. Although there is an operation for this purpose, called ventriculocordectomy, it is generally considered to be undesirable. It was developed and used primarily during the First World War as a means of preventing dogs, used in the trenches as messengers and for other activities, from betraying their positions by a casual bark.

Under normal domestic circumstances barking can be controlled without such mutilation being necessary. If you do suspect that your dog does bark excessively in certain situations, while waiting in the car for example, it may be worthwhile speaking with your vet. Often in such circumstances, it may have been that the dog was teased in the past, by a stranger who encouraged it to bark by tapping repeatedly on the window, for example.

Although you may not be able to track down the precise cause under such circumstances, it can be possible to devise a means of overcoming the problem in most cases of this type. It may mean having to park in a car park, for example, rather than in a busy street where there are a lot of people passing by. Here the dog should be relatively quiet, because it will not feel threatened.

Guarding

Some breeds have been developed primarily for guarding livestock and property. Many of these, such as the Rottweiler and German Shepherd dog, are now popular as companion

dogs. Yet coupled with their loyalty these dogs are likely to have a latent hint of aggression in their natures. This is sadly not appreciated by many owners, and can become a cause of problems, which may sometimes even feature in the news headlines.

There is a particular risk that children could fall victim to the misplaced aggression of a guard dog. Under no circumstances should a young child be left alone with any dog, since there is inevitably a risk of conflict. Even a very trustworthy dog may turn on a person if it is being hurt or teased. Selective breeding can also greatly heighten the aggressive response in some dogs, with American Pit Bull Terriers having become notorious in this respect.

Aggression resulting from the dog's guarding instincts is manifested in various ways. Typical examples are attacks on postmen or aggression towards an owner when a toy or other item is removed from them. The problem can be exacerbated by a failure to teach the dog to give up items on command. Hormonal influences are important since this type of aggression is usually only apparent once the dog has reached puberty.

There is also a specific condition affecting some bitches called pseudo-pregnancy, which can result in displays of unexpected aggression. This results from an increased level of the hormone progesterone in the blood, which normally occurs as the result of pregnancy, but sometimes takes place without conception. The bitch may display all the typical signs of pregnancy, even to the extent of lactating, but actually has no puppies. Instead, she sees toys and other items, such as shoes and slippers, as her offspring. She will carry them around with her, and is likely to prove aggressive if you try to take them away during this phase. If your bitch is not neutered, you should be aware of the possibility of this behavioural change occurring soon after the time when she would normally have given birth, just over two months after her last heat. This phase should soon pass. There is a strong possibility, however, that phantom pregnancies will recur at successive heats. Spaying (sterlizing) may be the best long-term answer, especially if you have a young family, but hormonal treatment might be used when the symptoms first emerge.

LEFT
Dogs may prove to be fierce guardians of their home, but unprovoked displays of aggression cannot be tolerated. If you think that you may have a problem dog, seek specialist help before it injures someone.

According to a British study published in 1984, at least three-quarters of all dog owners look to their pets to provide some security around the home, but proper training is required to ensure that your dog does not become a dominant tyrant at home. Again, it will be much easier to achieve the desired response with a young puppy. While the sound of the doorbell or knocker can trigger the dog to start barking, this can be followed by aggression towards the caller.

You may want your dog to bark initially, to alert you to the fact that someone is at the door. As soon as you hear the dog barking though, you must tell it to be quiet, and make it sit away from the door. You should follow this by commanding the dog to 'stay' when you actually open the door. Apart from the risk of causing injury to your visitor, the dog might rush out into the road. This can be a particular problem with hounds, which tend to be less territorial than some other breeds.

LEFT
Here a dog is wary of a stranger, but does not move to attack. Unfortunately, puppies in particular may rush out through the door in this situation, often ignoring the visitor, and could end up on the road. Take care to avoid this possibility, training the dog to sit by the door.

RIGHT
Regular exercise off the leash will
help to prevent a young dog
from becoming destructive
around the home. Here a young
Labrador is retrieving an object
for its owner.

The simplest way to start is to encourage the dog to sit in the required position, even when there is no one at the door. You can then practise by sending another member of the family round to the front door to act as a visitor, making the dog sit again. Do not repeat this more than a couple of times in rapid succession however, because otherwise the dog may start to interpret this as a game. Once the dog sits readily at the sound of the doorbell, you can continue the process by opening the door.

If your dog persists in misbehaving when the doorbell is rung, then you may have to take alternative action. Shut the dog in another room, and leave it there for 10 minutes or so, as soon as it starts to be a problem. By being excluded in this way, it should soon learn to become more receptive when told to sit under these circumstances.

Commands off the leash

When you first allow your dog off the leash outside you should be confident that all the basic commands, especially the command 'stay' have been mastered by your pet. It is also important to choose a quiet locality for this purpose. Try to avoid an area where there are many other dogs being exercised, since they will inevitably prove a distraction. You may want to take your dog out earlier than normal if it is difficult to find a quiet spot. You must also choose an area where there is little traffic, with no busy roads nearby. If you do opt for a place in the countryside however, be certain that no farm livestock is in the vicinity either, as sheep especially may prove an irresistible subject of curiosity for dogs which have not encountered them before, and this can escalate to sheep-worrying.

It is usually a good idea to walk with your dog in the usual fashion at first, working through the basic commands. Then repeat the 'stay' command, having slipped off the leash. Call the dog to you, and encourage it to walk with you for a distance before repeating the process. It is likely that at some stage the dog will run off some distance away.

The one thing never to do if your dog starts to stray from you is to chase off after it. Otherwise, it will think that you are playing a game, and will continue running, leaving you outpaced. Instead, stand still and call the dog back to you. Alternatively, you can call it to 'stay', but in the excitement of the moment and in strange surroundings, the dog may not comply. Again, wait a few moments before walking towards the dog, assuming it does stay, so as not to cause it to bound off.

A dependable means of retaining your dog's attention when it is first let off the leash is to take along a ball or flying disc. You can then encourage the dog to return to you without difficulty, by making a game which will entail the dog bringing the toy back. Do not be tempted to throw the toy too far ahead as this will be counter-productive. Always praise your pet when it returns to you on command.

You can also introduce a whistle to the training process at this stage. This can be especially useful if you are walking through an area with plenty of ground cover where you could lose sight of the dog. Special high frequency dog whistles are available for this purpose, which although virtually inaudible to the human ear, can be heard by dogs with their more sensitive hearing a good distance away.

It is a good idea to familiarize a dog to the sound of the whistle while it is still close to you. Establish a routine by calling the dog's name, and then giving a set number of blows on the whistle. Then even if you and the dog lose visual contact, the dog should hear the sound and return to you.

A dog which is being exercised off the leash will cover considerably more ground than if it is walking with you. In this early stage, once the dog is running free, you will probably find that it is more settled at home. This is because young dogs, from six months old, tend to need more exercise than other individuals. Nevertheless, aim to give the dog a good run every day, rather than undertaking a marathon at the weekend, for example. Excessive exercise can be damaging, especially for the giant breeds, particularly while they are still immature. In moderation, however, plenty of regular exercise will help to decrease the dog's

BELOW
You can develop the sit and stay routine with the dog off the leash, walking a considerable distance away before calling the dog to you. Always give plenty of praise when the dog sprints towards you.

destructive instincts around the home, as well as being essential for the smooth working of its cardiovascular system.

The dog will soon come to anticipate its walk eagerly, and rapidly settle into the routine of having a run before returning to you. There may be odd days, however, when a problem arises. The dog might pick up and follow a scent, before you are aware of this, and disappear into the distance. Continue the walk as normal, pausing for a time at the spot and call the dog back to you, rather than trying to pursue it. The dog should return within a few minutes, but if not, search in the direction where you last saw your pet. Repeated calling and whistling should entice the dog to return before long.

There is then little point in scolding the dog, and in fact this may well be counter-productive, because there is then less incentive for the dog to return in a similar situation if you become angry with it. The same applies if the dog returns with a dirty coat. This typically occurs just after you have given your dog a bath. Washing the coat removes the natural scent, which is important to the dog's status. As a result, it will seek an alternative pungent odour when roaming free out on a walk, and horse droppings and cow pats may prove irresistible. You should try to prevent this situation arising, possibly by exercising the dog on the leash for a day or so if it has shown a tendency to behave in this fashion in the past. Clearly, should this occur, you will have little option but to wash the dog again.

If you take the same walk every day, try to vary the routine, introducing and reinforcing training procedures, since this could be vital at other times. As stressed earlier, it is particularly important to persuade the dog to stay without any hesitation on its part. If you are on holiday with your dog, for example, you may encounter a canal or a similar stretch of water unexpectedly, and it will be important to ensure that your dog does not plunge into its depths, as this could be dangerous. Some breeds show a much greater desire to enter water than others, with retrievers tending to be especially keen. Aside from the fact that it may be difficult for the dog to get out of the water or escape from a strong current, the water itself might also be polluted, with equally serious consequences. Be as cautious with a dog as you would with a child.

Similarly, if you are on the beach, you should discourage your dog from drinking the water, or plunging straight into an area where the swell may be dangerous. People have died in such circumstances where a dog has leapt into the sea, encountered difficulties and then its owner has been swept away while trying to rescue their pet.

Before exercising your dog on the beach, you should check that this is permitted. In some areas, notably close to towns, dogs are banned from beaches. Always take a bowl and a bottle of clean drinking water for your pet so that it will not be tempted to drink salt water. Some dogs become very excited when they are first taken on the beach, so it may be advisable to keep your dog on its leash at first.

Again, when you do let it run free, try to choose a quiet spot away from people as much as possible. There is nothing more likely to cause ill-feeling than a large dog rushing through, demolishing a child's sandcastle or trailing sand through a picnic!

Another lesson which will need to be taught in these surroundings concerns pebbles. Some dogs appear to find them irresistible, although they show no interest in garden stones at home. Apart from the possibility of injuring their teeth quite badly by trying to gnaw them, there is also the distinct likelihood that some will be swallowed, causing an intestinal blockage. If your dog tries to pick up pebbles, you must command it to drop them before any harm results. It is much easier to prevent this situation developing by being firm from the outset, rather than trying to remedy it later. Playing with pebbles is unlikely to prove a novelty which will simply wear off.

RIGHT

Dogs often enjoy a run along the beach, but watch out for any traces of tar which could adhere to their feet or coat. If this happens remove as soon as possible, with a detergent.

LEFT

Water can mean danger, and you should always keep your dog on a leash, if there is any risk that it could fall in. It may otherwise be impossible to rescue your pet.

89

Toilet training outside the house and garden

While the general behaviour of some dogs on the beach can be a cause for concern, the main reason why they are banned from some beaches and other public places is because of the danger of contamination by their excrement. This is linked with particular concern over toxocariasis, since this disease can cause blindness in children. Clearly, it is most unpleasant to sit on the beach surrounded by dog excrement, and of course, above the high tide mark, it will remain here without being washed away by the sea.

Wherever you are out with your dog try to encourage it to defecate in a place where you can clean up easily afterwards. This is now compulsory in many public areas, and special disposal bins are provided for this purpose. You must be equipped with a cleaning tool and bag. A number of such products have recently been introduced to the market to make this task as straightforward as possible. Perhaps the most suitable types are those which can be carried easily in a pocket, and are entirely disposable. They obviate the need to walk about with a small shovel and separate bags.

Out in the countryside, rather than a public park, it is not essential to clear up after your dog. Under normal circumstances, with the dog running free, you may not even be aware of where it has defecated in undergrowth. Nevertheless, it is still advisable to train your dog to defecate on command as far as possible. Otherwise, you may not be aware of abnormalities associated with the passing of faeces, such as the presence of blood, which could be an important sign of illness.

Especially if you follow a similar path every day, then getting your dog to pass a motion will be easier to achieve by building on the previous training which it has received in home surroundings. Use the same command, preferably at a relatively early stage once the dog has settled down after being let out of the car, or off the leash. Do not forget to praise the dog when it performs on command. It should soon develop a habit of relieving itself in this way when it finds an appropriate spot at the start of its walk. Always make sure that your pet never fouls paths where people are walking.

When you are in a situation where you have to clean up after your dog it is advisable to encourage it to defecate on a surface which will make the task easier. Avoid areas where children are likely to congregate, since, inevitably, some traces of faeces will be left behind if the spot is not scrubbed. In any event you should ensure that your dog poses no threat to human health by deworming it every six months once it has reached this age. You can obtain suitable tablets for this from your vet and most pet shops.

FACING PAGE
When taking your dog to the 'great outdoors' – such as here, at the Chiricahua National Monument, Arizona – ensure that it relieves itself well away from footpaths and picnic areas.

BELOW LEFT
Dogs usually sniff carefully at the ground before deciding to relieve themselves. If the area concerned is not suitable, you should try to distract their attention elsewhere.

BELOW RIGHT
It can be considerably easier to clean up thoroughly after your pet if it relieves itself on a sandy surface, rather than on grass.

FOUR
TRAINING
DIFFICULTIES

TRAINING DIFFICULTIES

In spite of all your endeavours, there may be times when you encounter difficulties in the training process. Bear in mind that all dogs are individuals, and just because a previous dog learnt a command quickly, this does not mean that every individual has the same capacity. Certain dogs do appear to be more receptive than others.

Obtaining help and self-help

One of the advantages of attending training classes is that here you will be able to discuss your particular problems with an instructor in an atmosphere which is familiar to the dog. As a result, the cause of your concern may be more easily identified. It might be a failure on your part to adopt a consistent approach to training which is confusing the dog. In some instances, however, there could well be an underlying medical problem, which requires veterinary treatment. This is especially likely in cases where the dog is soiling its quarters, or showing signs of abnormal sexual behaviour, such as mounting your leg or that of visitors when they are sitting down.

Effective treatment obviously depends on isolating the cause, and if necessary your vet may recommend that in a particular instance a dog may benefit from assessment by an animal psychologist, specializing in behavioural problems. While general training serves to socialize the dog within the home and the community, there may be deviations from the usual pattern which can be rectified in this way. Most canine health insurance policies will

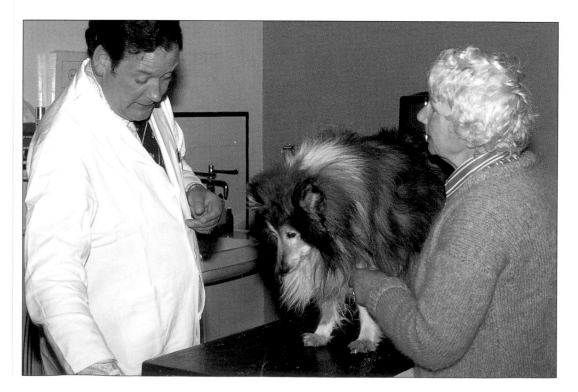

RIGHT

Vets can help with behavioural problems, whether or not these are a reflection of an underlying medical disorder.

LEFT
A secure muzzle should be fitted if your dog is likely to bite, when being examined by a vet, for example. Proper training from puppyhood should render this precaution unnecessary, but rescued dogs which have been mistreated in the past often remain very wary of strangers.

cover referrals of this nature if they are recommended by a qualified vet.

Displays of aggression are the most serious behavioural problem, both for the owner and others who come into contact with the dog. Never underestimate a dog's capability to inflict injury. Many people bear permanent scars from such encounters. You can, of course, invest in a stout muzzle, but this provides no real answer to this vice, since the dog will continue biting if it is given the opportunity.

There is no doubt that some dogs are naturally more aggressive than others, which is a reflection of their breeding. This is why breeds such as the Rottweiler and Dobermann need firm training right from the start, before they have a chance to challenge your authority. Male dogs tend to be worse in this respect than bitches, because they are naturally more dominant within a pack.

Aggression is not just confined to the larger breeds however, but can also be noted in the case of small dogs. Corrective measures are easier in this instance because of their size. You can pick up the dog and shake it, or pull on the scruff of its neck as happens when there is a clash over dominancy in the pack situation. Actually hitting a dog under these circumstances is likely to be counter-productive, however, as the dog may feel forced to challenge you again.

If you plan to go abroad, then clearly you will need to make arrangements for someone else to look after your dog while you are away from home. The ideal option is to have a friend or neighbour who is prepared to take your dog into their home for the duration. Here the dog will have the benefit of family companionship, but it is best to advise the person concerned not to let your pet off the leash when taking it for a walk outside. The dog might not respond readily to their commands, and may simply head off into the distance, possibly looking for you if the territory is familiar.

BELOW
Kennels usually have an indoor sleeping area, which is heated, and outdoor runs.

The other option to consider will be boarding kennels. Try to obtain recommendations for a good kennel in your area, either from breeders or possibly your vet. Then arrange to visit the kennels before making a definite booking, so that you can satisfy yourself with the standard of care. The runs should be clean, there should be an escape-proof entry system and the dogs themselves should look reasonably happy and contented. Do not be put off if some are howling. This is sometimes quite usual, especially if the dog concerned has just been left.

It is important to book as early as possible, since kennels fill up quickly at peak times, with customers booking from one year to the next. If you have trouble obtaining a reservation at a particular kennel, you can consider it a good sign. Ask whether you should take any items for your dog, such as a favourite sleeping blanket or toy.

If you are going abroad for an extended period, the other option is to take your dog with you. This depends largely on the quarantine situation. Whatever arrangements you make, however, you must ensure that the dog's inoculations are up to date. Kennels invariably require sight of a vaccination certificate signed by your veterinarian.

This should be checked again well in advance of your holiday.

If you are able to take your dog with you on holiday, remember that the area you are visiting will probably be unknown. It may be advisable, therefore, especially in the case of a young dog which is not yet fully trained to return when called, to keep your pet on the leash more than you would under normal circumstances. If the dog runs away, it may be much harder to find it here than at home. In addition, your schedule could be upset if you only intended to break your journey for a short time at a particular spot. You could find yourself having to stay in the area searching for your dog.

Some areas can hold hidden dangers for dogs. Avoid locations where there are abandoned mine shafts, which your dog could fall into and then become trapped.

These are often shown on maps. Walks on the beach also need to be undertaken with more caution if the tides are unknown. There could be strong currents, which represent a hazard if the dog enters the water. Bear in mind, too, the dangers of pollution.

While travelling, you will also need to make arrangements as to where your dog will sleep. Some hotels will accept dogs, but alternatively, if you have a large travelling cage, your pet may be happy to bed down here in the car, especially if provided with a favourite blanket. It is not advisable to give the dog free run of the car, however, simply because it could damage the interior, by scratching the upholstery, for example, if it wants to come out at first light before you are awake. It is difficult to prevent this sort of instinctive reaction.

An animal behaviourist can be of great value in cases of this type, helping you to reassert your dominance. A dog will generally give an indication of its intention to bite, by growling and curling its lips first. This is the stage to take decisive action, because by ignoring this threat gesture, you are merely acquiescing to the dog's challenge, and adopting a subordinate position. An effective way of dealing with this situation is to make the dog lie down, having first scruffed it by shaking its neck. A dog in this posture is subservient.

There may be specific events which promote aggressive displays in your dog, and such occurrences should be examined carefully. It may be grooming which triggers an outburst of this type. Under these circumstances, stop grooming the dog as normal, but instead switch this to a new locality. This places the dog at a disadvantage, and you can then regain the initiative and assert your dominance.

As has been mentioned previously, dogs which have been mistreated and passed through a number of other homes can represent a particular problem. In contrast to the dominant challenge situation, these dogs are being aggressive out of fear. Finding a remedy may be easier because there is less of a genetic component.

It is possible to distinguish between these different forms of aggressive behaviour by noting the body language of the dog concerned. In either case, the tail may be held very low, as may the head. But significantly, the ears are kept flat against the head when the dog is fearful, rather than being raised as in the case of a dominant gesture. Again, however, it is important to try to establish the cause of the condition, which is most common in the case of dogs which have not been properly socialized early in life. Alternatively, they may have been mistreated, and so only respond to that particular stimulus. This can explain why some dogs dislike an owner of one sex, or children, whom it associates with previous maltreatment.

Objects such as a shoe or slipper can also evoke this response if the dog was hit in the past. It is a sad fact that a number of adult dogs obtained from rescue organizations are returned because of this type of problem, which is not likely to be apparent when the dog is chosen. However, since this is a learnt response, conditioned by the object concerned, unlike dominance aggression it may be possible to ameliorate the dog's fear, although this will require time and patience on your part. You need to identify what precisely is upsetting the dog – is it all shoes, for example, or simply a particular type or colour? You can then plan to accustom the dog to the stimulus without conflict. If you encounter difficulties in this respect, do not hesitate to seek the advice of an animal behaviourist, since individual cases may benefit immensely from specific advice.

The general procedure, however, is to work with the dog over a period of time, ensuring a non-conflict situation so as to overcome its fears. The dog will associate the slipper with the pain of being beaten. You must be prepared to offer plenty of reassurance, therefore, at all stages in the process.

Start by wearing the slipper for periods, and ignore the dog at this stage. When you change your shoes, you should call the dog to you and then offer plenty of encouragement. This will serve to distract its attention from the slippers, which can be left around the home. Be careful not to lift the slippers off the ground when you put them on, however, as this is likely to cause the dog to become aggressive,

especially if it is effectively cornered in the room with you. Instead, simply slip off your shoes and slide your feet into the slippers. Again, you should ignore the dog, changing shoes without looking at it, by turning your back at this stage. This will minimize the perceived risk of conflict.

You should also call the dog to you when you are wearing the slippers and, assuming that it comes readily to you, make a fuss of it. Then when you are ready to take the dog out for a walk, you should again repeat the process, but now also change out of your slippers into shoes. Assuming that the dog remains with you, do not forget to give it plenty of encouragement again, as you attach the leash to its collar. In time the dog should come to accept your slippers without viewing them as a potential threat.

Similar routines can be developed in the case of other fears which dogs may acquire that lead to aggressive behaviour. Some individuals become excessively nervous about visiting the vet, for example, and it is a good idea to begin visits early in the dog's life. Puppies are naturally curious, and will not be afraid of visiting a vet, unlike an older dog. Taking them to the surgery for routine checks ensures that they should not associate this with unpleasant stimuli. Dogs are sensitive creatures, and they can detect your fear, if you are worried about the trip. In severe cases, they may respond by shaking and urinating uncontrollably when they come near the surgery. Then when the vet starts the examination the dog will become highly aggressive. Although it is possible to administer a sedative under these circumstances this is obviously not desirable for routine visits when the dog is not experiencing any pain.

Vaccines can usually be administered subcutaneously, that is, under the dog's skin, at the hindneck. This causes no discernible pain in the vast majority of cases. Indeed, the dog is often totally unaware of the vaccination. Injections into, say, the muscle of the hindleg

BELOW

For certain veterinary procedures, it may be less disturbing for your pet to be sedated, even though the operation itself may not be painful. Here a vet is removing an accumulation of tartar from a dog's teeth.

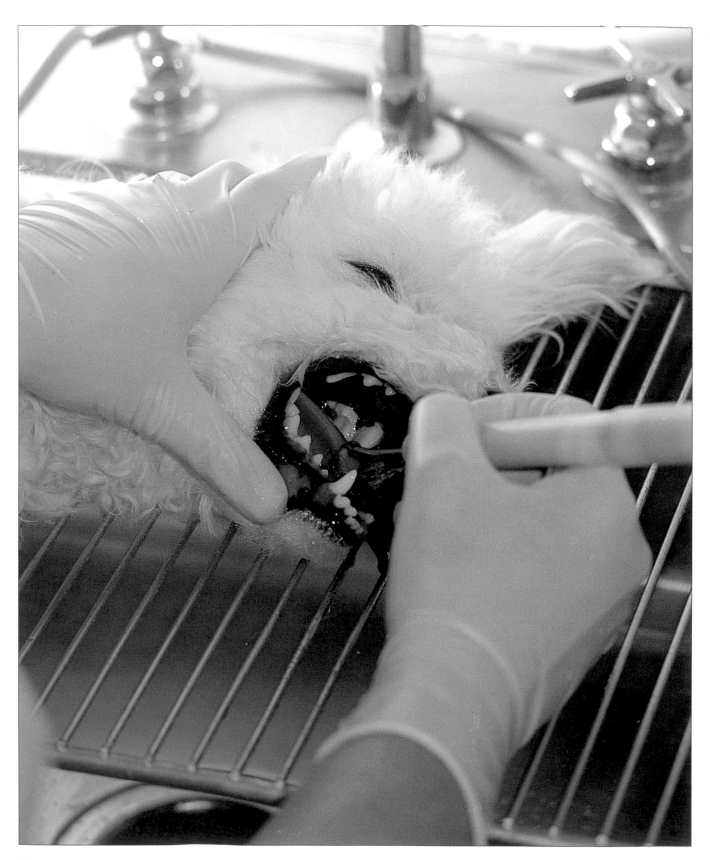

are more painful, but if you hold the dog as directed, offering plenty of reassurance, then no long-term behavioural problem should take hold as a result and the experience should be rapidly forgotten.

It is important to select a vet in whom you have confidence however, because if you are nervous and worried these sensations will be transmitted to the dog. In turn, it may well attempt to bite, and will then have to be restrained more firmly, perhaps by being muzzled. This may lead to problems in the future as a consequence. If your dog is somewhat possessive, it may be best if you leave the room while it is being examined. Discuss this with the vet beforehand so that a member of the staff can restrain the dog.

Few dogs actively appear to enjoy a visit to the vet, but conversely, even fewer normally become aggressive on routine visits if they are not in pain. When a dog does start to show signs of becoming difficult about a visit to the surgery, you may want to arrange with your vet simply to walk up to the waiting room, pause here for a few moments and then return home. Encourage the dog, giving plenty of praise at all stages. Once it realizes that going to the vet is not always an unpleasant experience, then its fear of this situation should be significantly reduced, and subsequently it should be easier for the dog to be examined without difficulty.

Some puppies, particularly around the time of teething, will start to play with your hand in their mouth. They may not bite as such but simply close their jaws around your hand for a few moments. This needs to be dealt with firmly however, before it escalates and leads to serious injury. Unfortunately, the action of pulling your hand away is likely to cause the dog to snap at you, in a bid to restrain your hand. Similarly, tapping the dog firmly on the nose may also persuade it that this is a game, and it will continue with such behaviour. Instead, you should respond by making the dog lie down, saying 'no' in a harsh voice and then ignoring it for a period, thus breaking off the

game. The dog will soon learn that this behaviour is unacceptable.

An adult male dog which tends to stray repeatedly and also soils indoors can present a major problem. There is always a risk that it will become involved in a road accident, and persistent soiling around the house will damage the furnishings. Speak to your vet about castrating the dog since the problems in this case are likely to be resulting from an excess of sexual libido.

Neutering reduces the incidence of straying in about 90 per cent of male dogs, and lowers the risk of soiling by decreasing the dog's sex drive. The operation described as

BELOW
There is plenty to interest a young puppy when it is out for a walk, but beware of hidden dangers. Rusty wire and broken bottles are obvious dangers, but snake bites are also a threat, and it is quite common for puppies to be stung by bees and wasps. They snap at the insect and catch it in their mouths while it is resting on a flower. Emergency first-aid may be required, as the tongue can swell up dramatically. Keep the tongue well forward, so that the entrance to the airways is not blocked.

castration is relatively simple, even in an older dog, because the incision is made in the testes, and there is no need to open the body cavity itself. Since the testes are removed, however, the dog will no longer be of value for breeding purposes.

Stealing

In spite of being well fed and cared for, some dogs will steal food and scavenge at every opportunity. This may lead owners to worry that the dog's diet is deficient in some respect, but if you are using a balanced prepared food, then there should be no concern about this. It is possible that there could be an underlying medical problem, however, especially if in spite of having a healthy appetite the dog appears to be losing weight.

Many owners prefer to feed adult dogs just once a day, but in fact, it may be better to offer food morning and evening, in smaller amounts. This can be less stressful for the dog, because its stomach will probably contain food for a longer period. On account of this it may be somewhat less prone to stealing, or consuming inedible objects such as stones.

Since they are scavengers by nature, in addition to their hunting instincts, many dogs will steal food even when they are being fed properly and are not suffering from illness. The simple solution in this case is to ensure that all food remains out of their reach. Be sure to

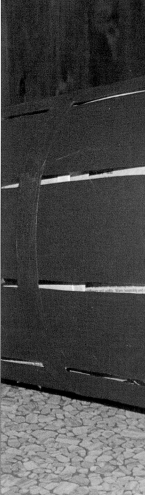

remember that as puppies grow up so they can reach higher, and the larger breeds can easily reach a worktop in a kitchen.

If you catch your dog in the act of stealing food, then you should scold it appropriately; after the event though, this is likely to be counter-productive. The dog will not be able to recollect the cause of the punishment, and as a result this may simply serve to damage the bond between you.

Even the scent of food, as on the wrapping around meat, can be attractive. If this is deposited in an open bin or refuse sack, the dog may steal the wrapping, taking it through the house, and causing a mess, as well as finally eating it. There is a possibility that this may cause a blockage in the intestinal tract,

while raw meat can be a source of various infectious micro-organisms, such as *Salmonella*.

Again, prevention is somewhat easier than overcoming the problem directly, but if you find the dog running off with something it has stolen from the rubbish, do not chase after it. The dog is likely to see this as a game, and a means of attracting your attention. Instead, call the dog back to you, and tell it to drop whatever it has taken. Do not scold the dog, but praise it instead, assuming that the item concerned is readily relinquished. Alternatively, you could open the dog's mouth and remove the item. The same applies if the dog takes other things such as slippers which it is not supposed to have, although it is equally important to replace them out of reach for the future.

LEFT
Do not discard food or food wrappings in waste bins, because your dog is unlikely to be able to resist the temptation of scavenging, tipping the bin out in the process.

TRAINING PROBLEMS WITH SPECIFIC BREEDS

If you are acquiring a cross-breed, try to establish its parentage as far as possible. This may have a bearing on the ease with which it can be trained. As a general guide, breeds which have been developed to work closely with people, such as retrievers, sheepdogs and spaniels are among the most responsive to training.

Hounds such as the Bassett can be particularly stubborn, especially about returning once they are off the leash. This relates directly to their ancestry; these short-legged hounds were bred to pursue their quarry by scent over considerable distances. This instinct still remains with these and similar breeds today.

Another dog which can prove difficult to train is the Chow Chow. This is a strong-willed and sometimes rather aggressive breed, which needs firm handling from puppyhood. Many of the training difficulties encountered with dogs in later life can be traced back to allowing them to exert a subtle dominance over you at any early stage, while they are puppies. This is why it is so important to be consistent in your approach right from the outset. The puppy will then settle in with relatively little difficulty as a member of the family. Otherwise, it will then become increasingly difficult to re-establish your authority at a later stage.

ABOVE
Greyhounds are lively, affectionate dogs, but are best muzzled when off the lead, as they retain their coursing instincts and may chase smaller dogs.

RIGHT
Though very lovable, the flat-nosed breeds, through selective breeding, have developed breathing difficulties. Such dogs, like this Pug, tend to overheat and many have actually suffocated in hot weather. The training process should therefore be modified accordingly.

The dog sees you as challenging its perceived dominance in the family arena, and may well turn on you when threatened, in the same way that it would a rival pack member which does not back down in the wild.

This can be one of the greatest difficulties to overcome if you take on an adult dog which has had several previous homes, and has gained a reputation for snappy behaviour. It is likely to challenge your dominance regularly at first. A combination of firmness and encouragement on your part can overcome the problem, and the dog may develop into a loyal companion. But such individuals cannot be recommended for a home with children. It is much better to obtain a puppy under these circumstances, which can grow up with you.

TOP RIGHT
Dobermans are strong individuals and can become dominant unless firmly trained from an early age. In the US great emphasis has been placed on rooting out aggressive instincts from those used for show stock, but this lead has not been followed so staunchly elsewhere.

RIGHT
This Norfolk Terrier may look like a 'toy' dog, but like all terriers it is a first-class ratter, and was developed as a working dog on farms. Bear in mind that mine shafts, burrows and all holes in the ground – with their attendant dangers – often prove irresistible to these breeds.

Problems with food

If a dog has a good appetite but seems to be losing weight, it may be suffering from a condition known as pancreatic insufficiency. This is frequently found in German Shepherd dogs (Alsatians).

Unless detected at an early stage weight loss is an inevitable result of pancreatic insufficiency, but before this becomes apparent the dog's appetite will have increased, simply because it is not absorbing enough nutrients. If you suspect that your dog could be suffering from this disease, consult your vet without

RIGHT AND BELOW
These photographs show extremes of obesity and emaciation. Aside from lack of exercise or food, however, underlying medical problems can cause excessive weight gain and loss. Your vet should be consulted as soon as you suspect that your pet could have a problem of this nature.

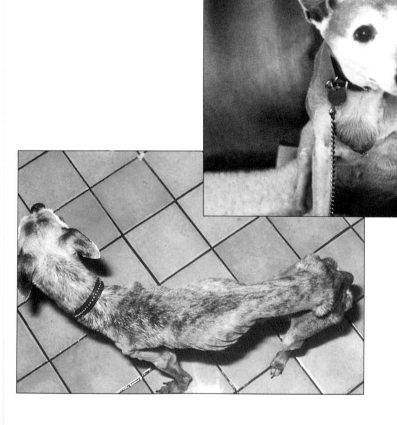

The pancreas is vital for digesting food, because it produces digestive enzymes as well as the hormone insulin. As the name of the disease suggests, there is an insufficient output, and so in turn food is not properly absorbed. The dog therefore receives less benefit than normal, with food passing in a relatively undigested state right through the digestive tract. The faeces in this instance tend to be relatively loose and pale in colour, while the dog remains hungry, simply because it cannot actually digest its food.

delay, so that appropriate treatment can be given. Early diagnosis will help to minimize the resulting weight loss which can be difficult to make up, even once the condition itself is being treated. The dog is given special tablets or capsules added to its food. Dietary modification may also be required, to raise the level of protein compared to the fat and carbohydrate content of the diet. You can buy special canned foods for this purpose.

A particularly unpleasant habit associated with food is that of coprophagia, or the eating of excrement. As has been mentioned previously, this tends to be encountered most commonly in dogs which have spent their early life in kennels. You will find this a difficult problem to cure, although medical help from your vet can be of value. A drug called cythioate, more usually administered to control fleas, imparts a highly unpleasant taste to the faeces, and this can be a suitable deterrent. Clearing up the faeces as soon as possible, whether in the garden or a park, is obviously to be recommended in any event, and this may help to break the habit. It is quite normal, however, for a bitch to consume the faeces of her pups, so do not be concerned in this case.

Studies have shown that the food preferences of dogs are stimulated by their early experiences. Therefore puppies housed after weaning in insanitary surroundings are at greatest risk from this vice. Some breeders recommend sprinkling faeces with an unpleasant substance such as curry powder, to act as a deterrent against coprophagia, but this is no substitute for keeping the dogs in clean surroundings.

Loss of appetite for other than medical reasons is quite rare in dogs. On occasions however, some individuals that are particularly fussy about their food may require encouragement to maintain their appetite in a strange place. Try to offer the dog's favourite food at this stage, and allow it to have its meals in quiet surroundings. Give words of encouragement, and do not take away the food immediately if it is ignored. The dog may well overcome its initial fear, and start to feed after a time on its own. If all else fails, consult a vet.

BELOW
Hand rearing . . . if a newborn puppy is unable to suck, it can be fed by way of a syringe.

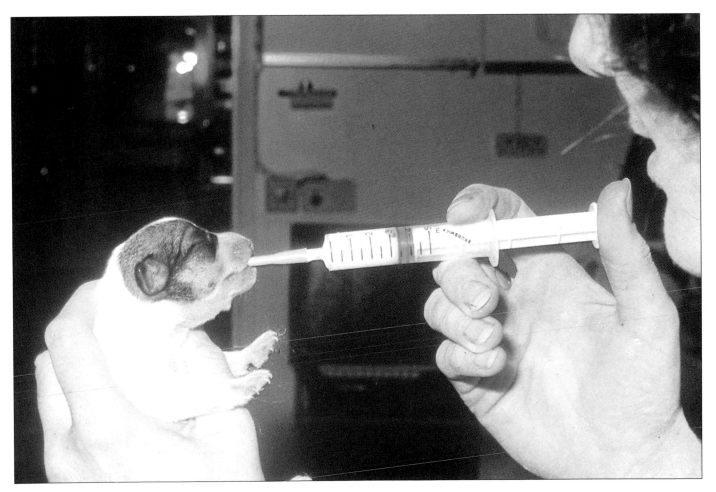

COMMON AILMENTS

Various ailments can interfere with the training schedule, and in some cases, you may not be aware of the actual cause. If your dog fails to respond readily over a period of time, it will be worthwhile having its hearing checked by a veterinarian. Congenital deafness is more commonly associated with some dogs than others – white boxers, for example, are prone to this condition.

Although there is no treatment, at least you can adjust your training routine accordingly. Otherwise, you may be misled into supposing that your dog is either being deliberately disobedient or simply stupid. Hand signals can be developed to a greater extent to train a dog which is deaf, although there is always the problem of attracting its attention in the first instance, particularly if it runs off. In such a case, it is especially important to establish a clear routine when you are exercising the dog. By sticking to the same route, your dog will become familiar with its surroundings, and will be far less likely to end up lost even if it strays away from you. Deaf dogs can manage surprisingly well, with their eyesight and sense of smell helping to compensate for their lack of hearing.

Not all hereditary ailments are apparent at birth, and one of the more serious is progressive retinal atrophy, often referred to under the acronym PRA. The retina itself is located at the back of the eye, and here the visual image forms, being transmitted to the brain via the optic nerve. In cases of PRA, the dog's vision fails progressively, with peripheral vision being affected first. This is a particular problem with working dogs, such as gundogs and collies, as they do not respond properly to their tasks; but in the home, pet dogs may not see objects around them, and start to appear abnormally clumsy. The earliest symptoms may be noted when dogs are working at dusk, but they are soon affected in daylight as well. An ophthalmic examination will reveal the cause of the problem, but there is no treatment available. Instead, extensive efforts are being made to eliminate the problem by screening breeding stock, such as Setters and Poodles, which are prone to this debilitating condition.

Another problem which owners may fail to appreciate at first is that when a dog is in pain, it may bite unexpectedly, even though the cause of the pain is not immediately obvious. Hip dysplasia is most commonly associated with large breeds, and puppies at just five months old may suffer pain from this condition. Should you attempt to pick up the dog, it is likely to howl and may attempt to snap at you. You

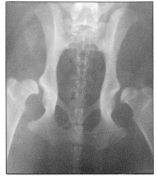

might at best have noted that the puppy had before been slightly lame. Under these circumstances, arrange for a veterinary examination. An X-ray picture should reveal the extent of the defect associated with the hip joints. Unfortunately, this is likely to become worse, although judicious use of pain-killers may overcome the worst effects.

You should avoid long runs, however, because these are likely to aggravate the condition. Surgery can sometimes assist, but again, the only long-term solution is screening of breeding stock. In turn, only buy puppies from breeders whose stock has been properly screened, whether for hip dysplasia or PRA, and these problems are unlikely to arise.

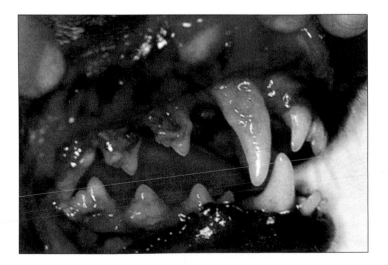

FIVE
DOGS
TOGETHER

DOGS TOGETHER

If you decide to keep more than one dog, you may decide to start with two puppies, so there is less risk of conflict, although this may entail a considerable amount of work. Bitches tend to be more compatible than dogs in most cases. Even so, it is usually possible to introduce another dog alongside an existing one satisfactorily, provided that you are aware of how the social structure operates within a group of dogs. There is a clear order of dominance in a pack, and dogs which have evolved to hunt in groups, such as beagles, are generally more amenable to the presence of a newcomer than those breeds which have been bred for a more solitary lifestyle, such as the Rottweiler – or, indeed, any guarding dogs with a strong territorial instinct.

In order to reduce the likelihood of aggression, you will need to maintain and reinforce the position of the established dog as the effective dominant individual when you acquire a new companion. Make more fuss of the first dog so that its position will not be threatened by the newcomer. Mealtimes are likely to be a particular source of conflict, and for this reason the dogs should be fed separately. Do not alter the feeding routine for your established pet, but feed the other dog elsewhere, preferably in a separate place.

Should there be an aggressive encounter between the two dogs, which is initiated by the established individual, do not scold this dog, as this will be perceived as a further challenge to its status. Always give your first attention to the established dog, and only subsequently acknowledge the newcomer. While this may seem somewhat harsh, it is vital to enforce the existing hierarchy at this stage. Otherwise, the situation will get out of control and conflict will be inevitable.

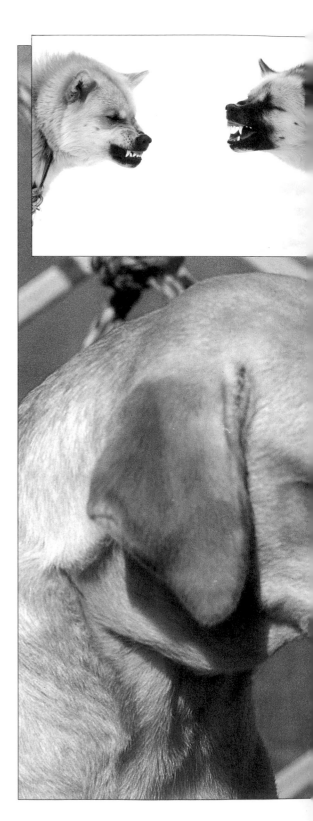

RIGHT AND INSET

For most dogs, a good-natured sniffing session is the best way of getting acquainted. Aggressive encounters between dogs are rare, since the subordinate individual usually backs down. Both, however, will make threatening gestures, such as snarling.

In our society today dogs perform a variety of tasks, aside from being kept as companions. They are still used in many parts of the world in their traditional role, of serving both to herd and guard farmstock. Nowadays, however, dogs also perform a much wider range of functions. Guide and sight dogs play a vital part in ensuring that many people with these disabilities can enjoy their lives much

more than would otherwise be possible. The use of dogs to scent explosives, in aircraft luggage, for example, has helped to make the world a safer place, as has the part played by dogs in combating drug smuggling.

While many people are happy just to own a well-trained dog, you may decide that you want to enter obedience competitions with your pet. Unlike dog shows as such, the entries in such cases are judged solely on the dog's individual abilities, rather than its type or appearance. Most dog training classes will give you greater insight into the requirements and methods used to ensure success at this high level of competition. Of course, even if you do not want to enter these shows, you can still benefit from the classes, which help to reinforce the bond between you.

Within the field environment, dogs have developed the special talents for which they were originally bred. The retrievers, for example, are a group of dogs which will find and bring back game after it has been shot. In contrast, the pointers will adopt their characteristic posture when they first detect the scent of game. Many other breeds have been kept and developed for sporting purposes, including numerous gundogs. These need steady and phlegmatic management if they are to reach their full potential, and offer specialist opportunities to enjoy the company of dogs, apart from as companions.

ABOVE
With their highly developed sense of smell, dogs are an indispensable weapon in the fight against drug trafficking.

LEFT
All gundogs, but especially Retrievers, are happy to go into the water to bring back their masters' quarry.

OPPOSITE ABOVE
The shepherd's complicated range of verbal commands and whistles helps the sheepdog to round up the flock inside a pen.

OPPOSITE BELOW
The bloodhound, given a sample of the relevant scent, can track down its quarry over a distance of several miles.

THE EVOLUTION OF DOG BREEDS

Many of today's 300 or so breeds were originally developed in particular countries of the world, for specific purposes in that area. Since then, many have become known to a wider dog-owning public. Keen breeders first usually arrange for the import of these new breeds, establishing a foundation stock in the new country. Although these dogs cannot be shown in their own classes at this stage, there are usually opportunities for them to be exhibited in mixed classes of rare breeds. Then if they prove popular, they are recognized by the governing canine authority and are allotted their own classes at shows, once sufficient numbers have been built up. It can therefore be a lengthy process to establish a new breed and then see it in the show ring.

As might be expected, a number of breeds have remained scarce, and achieved relatively little recognition among the dog-owning public at large. The popularity of a breed tends to rise and fall in accordance with fashion, but there will always be a dedicated core of breeders looking after its interests.

During recent years, the Hungarian breeds have become much better known outside the native land. Despite their long history – the origins of the Komodor date back over 1,000 years – they have been seen in the US only since the 1930s, and are even less common in Europe.

The appearance of the Komodor may not appeal to everyone, as they have a dense, corded coat. But this served to protect them from the climate, and enabled them to blend in among the sheep flocks which they guarded against wolves and other predators. It also helped to protect them from attacks by wolves.

The smaller version of the Komodor is called the Puli. This breed was used essentially for herding sheep, rather than defending them from attack. The traditional form of the Puli's coat is again corded, but in the combined interests of fashion and expediency, some breeders have encouraged owners to simply brush the coat Afro-style, rather than retaining the cords. Coat care in this case, as with the Komodor, is a lengthy process.

These utilitarian breeds lack the sleek appearance of the hunting dog of the

Hungarian nobles, known simply as the Vizsla, which translates as 'alert and responsive'. The native form of the Vizsla is smooth-coated and varies in colour from shades of sandy yellow through to gold. It was only during the 1930s, by which time the breed had become scarce, that the wire-haired form was produced. It involved the crossings of Vizslas with German Wire-haired Pointers.

These Hungarian examples give an insight into the development of breeds in other countries. There were those produced for looking after flocks, which called for bravery at a time when wolves and bears were far more numerous, especially in Europe, than they are today. Smaller breeds actually managed the livestock, while for recreation, the nobility bred hounds. As hunting patterns changed, and firearms became more reliable for hunting game, so gundogs, working either individually or in small groups, came into existence.

Today, the pet-seeker has a wider range of breeds, both ancient and modern, to choose from than at any stage in the past. But it is important to study carefully the history of any breed which you are thinking of choosing as a pet, to ensure that it fits into your lifestyle. Only in the last 100 years or so have dogs evolved away from their working ancestries to become primarily companion animals – and for some breeds, this transition has been more difficult than others.

Paying less attention to the newcomer can
be difficult, especially if you have young
children who are most likely to be attracted to
the new dog. It is important to explain to them
that their existing pet must be given attention
first, otherwise it will feel left out. Even with
two puppies of similar age, you should try to
identify the dominant individual, and plan the
training schedule accordingly. This will greatly
reduce the risk of conflict in the future, when
the dogs are older.

Should the dogs have a disagreement,
there is unlikely to be serious injury because
the subordinate individual will back down
almost immediately, when threatened by the
dominant dog. Only if there is a direct
challenge to the position of this individual is
fighting likely to be protracted. Nevertheless,
this depends to some extent on the breed, with
Bull Terriers, for example, tending to be
naturally aggressive towards each other, having
been bred originally for dog-fighting purposes.

As the weaker dog is likely to retreat after an aggressive encounter, the balance is likely to be restored. Even after a skirmish of this type, the consequences will be short-lived, and there is no need to fear that you will have to keep the dogs separated for the rest of their lives. Similar encounters are common in packs of wild dogs, and serve to establish the order of dominance. They do not imply that one dog is aggressive compared with the other.

While this may suggest that keeping two dogs together is a source of potential conflict, the truth is that a balance is soon established, even between dogs of different ages. A young dog can help to rejuvenate an older individual, while the dogs will benefit from the companionship of the other when you are out. Watching them together will be a source of great delight. But remember that continual friction is ultimately the trainer's fault.

LEFT
Once the newcomer is settled, the two dogs will play happily together, without any signs of aggression. The new arrival usually assumes a subordinate role.

Introduction of a new dog

In the canine world, scent marking is an important means of communication, and when a new individual is acquired, there may be an apparent breakdown in the toilet training of the established dog. In reality, however, this tends to be related to the stress induced by the intrusion of the newcomer. This situation is worse in the case of male dogs. This is because they have a higher level of the male sex hormone, called testosterone, in their circulation, which serves, amongst other functions, to stimulate territorial marking with urine.

Perhaps not surprisingly, such behaviour is unlikely to become apparent much before puberty, and peaks in young dogs between their second and third year. This phase should pass as the order of dominance is reasserted, but if it persists, then rather than punish the dog for what is a natural reaction to an incursion on to its territory, you should discuss the problem with your vet. Castration of both dogs can be advisable under these circumstances. This will certainly reduce the level of soiling indoors, and hopefully eliminate it entirely in these surroundings.

For a shorter-term option, however, the use of a progesterone-type drug may resolve the problem, allowing the dogs to become better acquainted in this time. If you catch the dog spraying indoors, you can treat it as outlined earlier with regard to toilet training, but it is most unwise to react at a later stage. This will be perceived as a further attack on its status, and the cause will not be appreciated, and consequently the situation can inadvertently be worsened.

There can be times when dogs, either living in groups or on their own, may become more aggressive or excitable than normal. This often occurs before a thunderstorm. Dogs are able to detect the sounds of the storm before these are audible to our ears, and will become scared. In severe cases, you may need to obtain sedatives from your vet, especially if you live in an area where thunderstorms are a fairly regular occurrence. Alternatively you may want to try to desensitize your dogs by recording the noise of a storm, and then playing this back to them. Start at a low volume, giving plenty of encouragement, and provided that the dogs do not become distressed, you can increase the volume somewhat. Repetition and making a fuss of your pets, effectively distracting their attention at first if they start to become nervous, should overcome the problem over a period. Time spent on this activity will not be wasted, especially if you have the misfortune to be caught out in a storm with the dogs. The last thing which you will want at this stage is for them to run off in opposite directions through fear.

BELOW

You will need to feed the dogs separately, to avoid possible conflict over food. The garden can be useful for this purpose, as it is easy to separate the dogs without any risk of aggression at mealtimes.

Exercise

Under normal circumstances when they are being exercised together, the dogs will probably remain quite close to each other, especially if they are naturally pack hounds. It can sometimes be difficult to train the newcomer without threatening the established routine which you have built up with your first dog. In the early stages therefore, you may prefer to exercise the dogs separately so there is no risk of conflict. Certainly, the newcomer should never be let off the leash before the basic commands have been mastered in the hope that it will simply follow the example of the older dog. While this may occur to some extent, there is also a strong possibility that the dogs will head off and go their separate ways. The newcomer may disappear into the distance and prove almost impossible to catch up, if it has not had a sound basic training.

If you are taking the dogs out for a walk on the leash, it is still advisable to keep them both on your left-hand side, rather than holding a leash in each hand. This emphasizes a consistency of approach, and with larger dogs, prevents you from being pulled in two possible directions, blocking the pavement as a result. It may be helpful to fit the bigger breeds with harness-type leashes, which can give you more control over their movements. Do not underestimate the power of these larger dogs if they choose to pull while on the leash. You could find it a major struggle to restrain both dogs effectively.

Exercising the dogs on neutral territory is a good way for them to become acquainted with each other without friction. Even dogs which have never met each other before will frequently walk happily together without any signs of conflict when they are outside their domestic environments. Problems may arise if you decide subsequently to play a game with them, and there is only one ball, for example. Always encourage the dominant dog to chase

after it first, and then allow the other dog to participate in the game. While it is possible for two dogs to chase the same ball without conflict, there is a real possibility that this could lead to fighting, especially if the normally dominant individual is slower to reach the scene of the action.

Sexual behaviour

The sexuality of their pet can be a problem for all dog owners, but is probably heightened when two dogs are kept together, especially if they are of the opposite sex. The majority of male dogs reach puberty between six and 12 months old, but are rarely used for breeding before the age of a year. The female dog has a much more restricted breeding phase than her male partner, who can mate at virtually any stage during the year. It is usual for bitches to mature slightly earlier than dogs, although this depends to some extent on the breed.

Your bitch will have one, or more usually two, periods of sexual activity, frequently

ABOVE

Dogs which have been reared together form a natural pack, and a puppy which grows up with one or both of its parents will live happily alongside them.

121

described as 'heats' or 'seasons', each year. These are accompanied by significant behavioural changes. During the first stage of heat, described as pro-oestrus, she will become more playful than normal, yet rebuff the attentions of male dogs which venture too close, even to the point of being aggressive.

At this stage, there will be a bloody discharge apparent from her vulva. As this ceases, so the time for mating approaches, and it is particularly vital to keep the bitch away from intact males at this time. Chemical messengers, called pheromones, will attract males to the area, knowing that she is ready to mate. You should keep her indoors, and only exercise her under supervision in your garden at this stage. Apart from the risk of male dogs gaining access, there is also a real possibility that the bitch herself may go to great lengths to escape, in order to find a mate.

You cannot rely on training at this stage to prevent an unwanted pregnancy. Nor will the bitch be able to control the discharge from her vulva, which is likely to be deposited around the home, on carpeting or furniture if she is allowed to sleep here. Heat can therefore be a troublesome period, which lasts about three weeks on average.

If you keep male dogs, and there is a bitch on heat in the vicinity, you may well find that the dogs disappear, in spite of their usually good behaviour. Again, there is virtually nothing you can do by way of training to prevent such instinctive responses, but you should aim to discourage the dogs from wandering off by supervising them closely.

Dogs should only be allowed to mate if they are healthy and the resulting puppies can be assured of good homes. Sadly, this is not always the case, and many dogs continue to be destroyed each year as a result. While it is possible to use drugs to prevent a bitch from conceiving at a particular season, the operation popularly known as 'spaying' will ensure that she will not have puppies in the future. Spaying, more technically described as an

ovariohysterectomy, entails the removal of both the ovaries and the uterus through the wall of the abdomen. It is normally carried out when the bitch is not in season.

Having decided to spay your bitch, do not allow her to run around excessively for the first few days after surgery, and exercise her on a leash at this stage. The wound should heal rapidly and the stitches can be removed 10 days later. You may find that the bitch then tends to put on weight quite readily, so you will need to reduce her food intake gradually, and ensure that she has adequate exercise.

While a female dog's sexual activity is confined to just a few weeks of the year, behavioural problems can arise with males, especially puppies, around puberty, and become persistent. If kept with other dogs, they may try to mount them, or else a dog may climb on to your legs, usually when you are sitting down in an armchair. Such behaviour may also be encountered in bitches, but is generally far less common.

In either case the remedy should be the same, with the dog being made to lie down when it is about to mount your leg. This will distract it as well before the behaviour becomes habitual. If you find the dog climbing on to the chair arm, the response should be the

A whelping box should be provided for the bitch well before the puppies are due. It should be placed in a dark, quiet and draught-free place and preferably raised slightly off the ground. Even if the bitch does not choose to use the box for whelping, after birth she and the puppies can be moved there. A playpen can be attached to the front of the box later on when the puppies start to venture out.

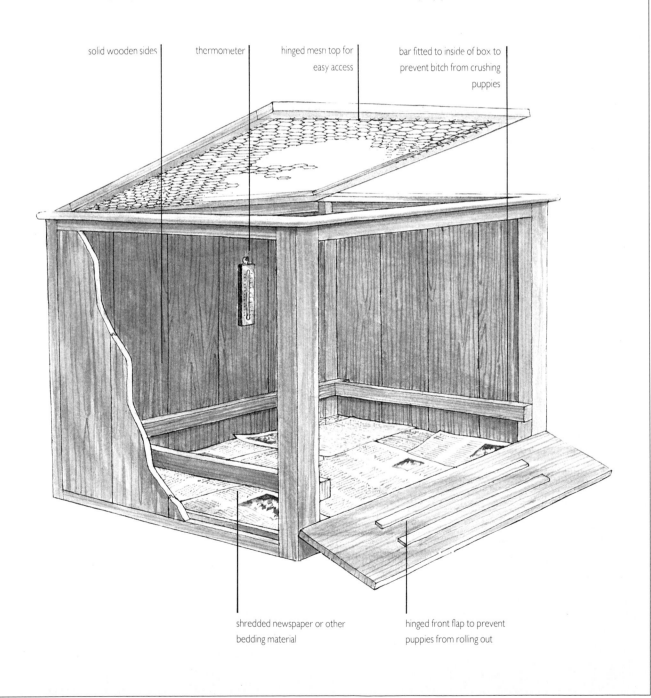

solid wooden sides

thermometer

hinged mesh top for easy access

bar fitted to inside of box to prevent bitch from crushing puppies

shredded newspaper or other bedding material

hinged front flap to prevent puppies from rolling out

same. You should otherwise avoid any contact with the dog, so as not to allow this to develop into an attention-seeking ritual. Confine the dog for a few minutes on its own whenever it tries to behave in this way and the phase should soon pass. Otherwise, you may find yourself faced with a major problem. As an example, owners of a Dachshund began by having to confine their dog on 84 occasions for this reason on one day alone, although within three weeks the problem had been resolved.

problems which may have a hormonal basis. Aside from reducing the desire to mate, both normally and abnormally, it should also help to prevent the dog from straying. The dog's level of aggression may similarly be reduced, and there should be fewer accompanying signs, such as urine spraying around the home. Yet otherwise, it is unlikely to alter the personality of the dog, or its level of excitability. You must watch a castrated male's weight, however, because obesity can then occur quite rapidly.

FACING PAGE

Even before your bitch becomes pregnant, remember that it may not be easy to find homes for all the puppies. There are already many unwanted dogs turned out on to the streets, and you should avoid any risk of adding to the numbers. Try to find good homes, therefore, even before you mate your bitch.

LEFT

Avoid interfering unnecessarily with young puppies. The bitch may be very protective towards them, especially in the early stages after giving birth, and may actively resent your intrusion.

With a male dog in the longer term, you may want to consider castration if you have no intention of breeding with it. Like spaying, this is not a reversible operation since it entails removal of the testes themselves. Castration can help a number of separate behavioural

But whether or not you decide to opt for a pure-bred (pedigree) or a cross-bred, there is no substitute for properly training your dog from the start, so that it will become a pleasant and reliable member of the community.

INDEX

Captions to illustrations are indicated by *italic* page numbers.

PICTURE CREDITS

r = right; l = left; b = bottom; t = top

Norvia Behling: 6, 8, 9, 13, 24, 29, 33r, 34, 38, 52, 53, 54, 56, 62, 81t, 88b, 90, 92, 102,
110, 112–13, 120; Marc Henrie: 10, 11b, 12, 14, 15, 16, 17, 18, 19t, 20, 21, 23, 25, 27, 33l,
35, 40, 43, 45, 46, 47, 50, 55, 59, 60b, 65, 66, 67, 68, 69, 70b, 72, 73, 74, 75, 76, 78t, 80,
82, 83, 85, 86, 87, 88t, 94, 96, 97, 98, 105b, 109tl, 114, 115, 116, 118, 119, 121, 124;
Spectrum Colour Library: 11t, 28, 32, 64, 104, 105t, 109b, 122; Sally Anne Thompson:
19b, 60t, 84, 117b, 125; Kent and Donna Dannen: 22, 30, 36, 37, 39, 41, 42, 48, 57, 61,
70t, 77, 78b, 81b, 91, 95, 103, 104, 105; Trevor Wood: 26; Quarto Publishing Limited:
70; Mandeville Veterinary College: 106, 107, 109tr; Ardea, London: 112 (inset); Terry
Smith: 117t.